Contents

Part III – On Art and Life

Furtwängler on Music

Essays and Addresses

edited and translated by
RONALD TAYLOR

Scolar Press

Published by
SCOLAR PRESS
Gower House
Croft Road
Aldershot
Hants GU11 3HR
England

Gower Publishing Company
Old Post Road
Brookfield
Vermont 05036
USA

This publication received financial support from Inter Nationes

British Library Cataloguing in Publication Data
Furtwängler, Wilhelm *1886–1954*
    Furtwängler on music.
    1. Music
    I. Title   II. Taylor, Ronald
    780

    ISBN 0–85967–816–4

Phototypeset by Intype, London
Printed and bound in Great Britain by
Billing and Sons Limited, Worcester.

Introduction

There is no reason why we should expect a musician – or any other artist whose medium is not that of words – to pick up a pen and express his opinions on the development of his art and the problems that confront it. A composer speaks in music, not in language, so does the performer of that music. Beethoven found no need to put on record his perception of the evolution of the symphony, or what he had in mind with his radical changes to that form. Michelangelo did not compile a notebook of observations to be held in the hand while looking at a Pietà or the tombs of the Medici.

The Romantic nineteenth century thought differently. The rise of subjective supremacy was accompanied by a feeling that the new emphases and values needed to be made explicit. Weber, Schumann, Liszt, Wagner – all expressed themselves at length, sometimes exorbitant length, on the music of their predecessors and contemporaries and on the directions in which music was moving – or, in the case of Liszt and his son-in-law, was being propelled. Richard Strauss too, headman of the German Romantic epigones, had plenty to say on the musical world in general.

Then, in the Modernist decades of the early twentieth century, theories of music, from being commentaries and analyses of the music in which primacy lay, cast off their parasitic role and took over the centre of the stage, issuing prescriptive statements on the true way forward. The revolutionary twelve-tone movement loomed large, appearing to offer a way out of the alleged state of crisis at which 'traditional' music had arrived. A scheme of composition in quarter-tones was put forward. And with changes in social structure and balance came questions about the relationship between art and society and about the social responsibility of the artist.

This interlocked with what had always been a powerful concern of German thinkers in particular, namely the didactic quality of art, art as a medium for inculcating values – moral, political, social, aesthetic – in the individual mind, thence in the consciousness of society and ultimately in the self-awareness of the whole nation. History, philosophy, sociology, anthropology were drawn into the aesthetic argument, theories and counter-theories were flung to and fro, stances were struck, intellectual games played. Few now chose, or were able, to keep out of the firing line for long, or declined the invitation to answer 'Present' when their particular roll was called.

Performers also had something to contribute, if more often in the form of reflections and reminiscences than of theories and analyses. And among the ranks of interpreters it is perhaps the conductor, in concert hall or opera house, confronting the public, the critics and the captains of the music industry, who has the most natural right to comment on what he sees – on his relationship to particular composers and works, on aspects of performance, on developments in theory and technique, on the musical state of health of *urbs et orbis*.

A conductor who felt that he had this right – he would have called it a duty – and whose influence was all the greater for his being one of the great conductors of the twentieth century, was Wilhelm Furtwängler.

Furtwängler's life, personal and professional, was as full of vicissitudes as the history of the years it spanned. He was born in Berlin on 5 March 1886, the eldest of four children. The family, Protestant by faith, enjoyed a comfortable middle-class existence. Adolf Furtwängler, Wilhelm's father, was a Classical archaeologist who founded his considerable reputation on exca-vations of the site of Olympia in 1878.

The Furtwängler household breathed culture and knowledge of every kind. But Adolf believed in an education based on an individual spirit of enquiry, not on the discipline of the class-room, and when Wilhelm was thirteen, he took him away from grammar school and engaged two private tutors to provide him with a blend of formal exercise and the encouragement of per-sonal initiative. It was a form of education that consolidated, perhaps even helped to shape, the independent, inward-look-ing, self-dependent character which he showed from childhood and which dominated his public image as man and musician.

Music came into 'Willi's' life at an early age. His mother gave him his first piano lessons, and his precosity survives in the form of a quaint little ditty, inscribed 'A Little Piece about the

Animals', that he sketched when he was seven as a birthday present for his father. Other little pieces followed, strengthening year by year the conviction, which never left him, that his vocation was that of a composer. He had a few spells of tuition in theory and composition as a teenager, among others from the organist Joseph Rheinberger and the composer Max von Schillings, but in essence he learned what he wanted from the direct inspiration of great minds, in music – Bach, Beethoven, Haydn, Mozart, Schubert – as in literature and philosophy – the Greek and Roman Classics, Shakespeare, Goethe, Kleist, Kant.

At nineteen he was offered his first professional post, that of repetiteur at the Stadttheater in Breslau. He did not take to the humdrum work and the discipline it imposed. Nor did he enjoy the disastrous reception given there to a performance of his first orchestral work, a Symphony in D. Stung by this failure, he arranged, with his father's help, for a concert to be given in Munich the following year, 1906, when he would conduct another of his early compositions – a symphonic Adagio movement. The programme also included Bruckner's Ninth Symphony, no less – this, to mark the début of a young man who had had no lessons in conducting and never stood in front of an orchestra before. Furtwängler did not do things by halves.

But the occasion turned out to be a considerable success, the novice conductor achieving by force of personality and commitment what most would have said required at least a modicum of technical expertise. The evening belonged, however, to Furtwängler the conductor rather than Furtwängler the composer – a circumstance which may give us little cause for surprise but which for him was a sore disappointment.

After a year in Breslau he took a succession of similar one- and two-year jobs in Zürich, Munich and Strasbourg until, in 1911, a first really substantial opportunity came his way – the conductorship of the orchestra of the Society of the Friends of Music in the venerable Hanseatic town of Lübeck. The self-taught technique of the tall, lanky, willowy Furtwängler – or the lack thereof – caused considerable consternation, yet the end seemed to justify the means. 'It must be admitted,' wrote an observer,

> that Furtwängler's outward gestures are indescribably comic. He waves his arms about like a windmill and makes the most horrible grimaces. His legs make their own independent movements, and

the overall impression is one of utter confusion. But when the sound of the music reaches one's ears, all is forgiven and forgotten. . . . At the end the applause is deafening. Thoughts of being the first to collect one's hat and coat from the cloakroom, or of rushing off to catch the last train or tram, simply do not enter one's head. People just stand there, clapping wildly until their hands hurt.

There was one conductor, and one alone, whose example inspired him. This was Arthur Nikisch, conductor of both the Berlin Philharmonic Orchestra and the Gewandhaus orchestra in Leipzig. Nikisch's hypnotic control over his players – 'a mysterious spell', Tchaikovsky called it – was exercised with utter calm and a minimum of movement, the perfect antidote to Furtwängler's flailing of arms and excited leaps. Furtwängler never lost his admiration for the beauty of sound that Nikisch could coax from an orchestra like no other (see 'The Tools of the Conductor's Trade,' pp. 16ff below).

In 1915, after four years of orchestral and choral conducting in Lübeck, Furtwängler was invited to return to the world of opera as Kapellmeister in Mannheim, a town with a great tradition in music and drama. Ambitious though he was, big leaps forward in his career, like this, were preceded by hesitancies and doubts on his part. Nor did he enjoy the social obligations which beset the life of a public figure, which he found the more oppressive the more his fame grew. Instead of holding court in his dressing room after the performance and receiving the congratulations of his well-heeled audience, he would have preferred to leave the theatre quietly on his own, walk back through the dark streets to his apartment, then take a stroll along the banks of the Rhine with his dog, reflecting on the evening's music. He once described himself as 'a badger who likes to crawl back to his set'.

The operatic range that Furtwängler developed during his five years at Mannheim took in the basic eighteenth- and nineteenth-century German repertoire – the five core Mozart works, *Fidelio*, *Der Freischütz*, Wagner from *Der fliegende Holländer* to *Parsifal* – and a number of now less well-known pieces such as Marschner's *Hans Heiling*, Max von Schillings' *Mona Lisa* and Pfitzner's *Der Arme Heinrich*, a total of thirty-four productions in all. 'I am gradually becoming a good conductor,' he wrote to a friend, adding rather sourly: 'The people here are a pretty boring lot but I have a feeling – and I hope I am right – that as I get older, I shall reach the point where I am totally relieved of such needs.' Furtwängler the thirty-year-old misanthropist. He did indeed find it hard to derive much pleasure from the company of more than a handful of his fellow-men, the manifestation of a curious blend of intellectual self-sufficiency, emotional insecurity and a deep unwillingness to admit that he 'needed' anyone else.

Furtwängler was not called up for military service and stayed in Mannheim until the end of the 1919–20 season. The following year he freelanced. Then, at the beginning of 1922, Nikisch died suddenly at the age of sixty-six. What Furtwängler had secretly dreamt of, perhaps even considered to be what a rational fate would decree, now became a reality – both Nikisch's permanent positions were offered to him.

His acceptance brought him to the threshold of the dozen or so years that marked the zenith of his career, in terms both of public acclaim and of inner fulfilment. In the same year as he moved to Berlin, he conducted his first concert with the Vienna Philharmonic Orchestra, launching an association that lasted, like that with the Berlin Philharmonic, to the end of his life. Two years later, in 1924, he came to London for the first time, and was invited the following year to give a series of ten concerts with the New York Philharmonic Orchestra (this was a year before Toscanini gave his first concert with that orchestra – a circumstance Toscanini was none too keen to be reminded of). Not that he was without his rivals in Germany – Bruno Walter, Mengelberg, Klemperer, Kleiber, Weingartner – but they could not reach the pre-eminence he enjoyed through the power of his official positions. Even after resigning from the Gewandhaus in 1928 under the growing pressure of his commitments, he still found himself conducting over one hundred concerts a year.

Conductor *par excellence* in the Romantic manner, Furtwängler viewed music from a firm nineteenth-century platform of Beethoven, Wagner, Bruckner and Brahms. His whole scheme of values, moral and social as well as musical, was based on what nineteenth-century German music stood for – its idealism, its faith in an absolute, all-pervading nature, its frank expression of emotion, its assumption of a community of interest between artist and public as the context of all artistic activity. His philosophy of music was a philosophy of life. True art ennobles the soul, enhances the sensitivity of mind and emotional consciousness, and serves the holistic education of man's emotional, mental and spiritual faculties. On the promotion of such humanist values, as he saw them, depended the survival of a sane world and a healthy culture. This is the spirit that informs his various essays and addresses.

But for all his devotion to the Classical tradition, Furtwängler was not deaf to the music of his own day. There were few modern composers to whom he felt temperamentally drawn but he recognized quality when he saw it. Scriabin, Schoenberg (he gave the first performance of the Variations for Orchestra Op. 31), Bartók, Honegger, Stravinsky's *Rite of Spring* (whose irregular metres Klemperer confessed he could not beat), Hindemith (the première of the *Mathis der Maler* symphony) – this is a selection of the music he championed. Hardly the evidence on which to rest a case of Furtwängler as reactionary *laudator temporis acti*.

In 1923, the year after his twin appointments to Berlin and Leipzig, Furtwängler married his first wife, a Danish woman two years his senior called Zitla Lund. They made their home in Berlin and Furtwängler also bought a house in St Moritz, but although they remained married for twenty years, the relationship did not have the intimate contact of minds which he needed in anyone with whom he was to share even part of his life. He was a strenuous companion, on the one hand self-denying, brooding over the fate of music and the world, on the other a lover of natural pleasures, especially of the outdoor life, an indefatigable mountain walker and a keen skier. The disciplined, almost humourless intellectual struggling with a philosophy of art gives way to a love of theatre and spectacle, the correlative of the full-blooded Romantic sonority that he drew from his orchestras. Above all he was a great lover of children, but Zitla bore him none. It was not until his second marriage in 1943, by which time he was approaching sixty, that he was able to act out his favourite role as paterfamilias to the full.

As the Weimar Republic tottered towards its final disintegration and the shadow of Hitler grew longer, signs of uncertainty began to enter Furtwängler's life. He was forced to make an unwelcome decision between Berlin and Vienna, both of whom wanted him for their orchestras; there was trouble with Winifred Wagner over the nature of his association with Bayreuth. But dwarfing these domestic squabbles were the implications of the events of January 1933, when Hitler acquired absolute power as Chancellor of Germany. The anti-Semitism on which Nazism fed received the status of law, with the corresponding punishment of those who disobeyed. One declared aim of the legislation was to drive Jews out of public life – including, of course, the arts, which could not exist without a public. And the number of Jews active specifically in music – leading figures like Schoenberg, Kurt Weill, Bruno Walter, Klemperer, Schnabel, Hubermann, Leo Kestenberg, not to speak of the hundreds of rank-and-file players in orchestras up and down the country – was prodigious.

Up until then Furtwängler had paid little heed to political developments. But when, as conductor of the country's leading orchestra, he was told that it was his patriotic duty to get rid of the Jews among his players, and in particular of Berta Geissmar, the faithful Jewish secretary he had had since his days in Mannheim, he became indignant. He did not see the anti-Semitic crusade as evil, or wicked, or obscene but as stupid, senseless, an irrelevance and an inconvenience. When he protested to Goebbels (see his 'Open Letter' p. 138 below) – and we must not forget that he *did* protest – it was in the name of music, not in response to a feeling of revulsion or horror or to an unconditional moral imperative. He was perilously close at this moment to that most mortal of sins – doing the right thing for the wrong reasons.

The question of Furtwängler's relationship to the Nazis was to cloud the rest of his life. He was no Nazi. He intervened for as long as he could on behalf of his Jewish musicians and refused to dismiss Berta Geissmar, who stayed with him until the Nuremberg Laws of 1935 forced her into exile. In 1934 he took up cudgels on behalf of Paul Hindemith, who was the subject of a Nazi smear campaign. He refused to conduct at Nazi party rallies, resigned from the newly-founded Reichsmusikkammer and gave up the directorship of the Berlin State Opera.

By actions such as these he tried to prevent the complete politicization of music in the Third Reich. He even thought, in his political naiveté, that he could do something to influence the situation for the better, if not politically, then at least for art, for music. However innocent – many called it childish – his belief may have seemed, it was one of the main reasons why he did not emigrate. And if, after a gala performance of Beethoven's Ninth Symphony in Berlin the Führer leapt up from his seat in the front row and enthusiastically shook his hand, how could the victim prevent the press photograph from being flashed round the world as proof of his identification with the regime? How, asked the enraged Toscanini, could one have the effrontery to conduct Beethoven in a Fascist state and still maintain one had a clear conscience?

In 1943 and 1944 he conducted *Die Meistersinger* at the famous wartime Bayreuth Festivals attended by servicemen. Also in 1943 he married for a second time – one Elisabeth Albert, widow of an army officer who had been killed in France in 1940. She already had four children; Furtwängler had five, by various short-lived liaisons before and during his marriage to Zitla. He and Elisabeth later had their own son, and they both, in a touching spirit of union and affection, came to love all ten children as one indivisible family during the eleven years of their life together.

As the end of the war approached, the bizarre nature of Furtwängler's position became starkly apparent. Although he seemed to have been able to steer a path between submission and open defiance, he could never be sure of his survival, and shortly before the German collapse he and his family sought refuge in Switzerland. But he was by no means *persona grata* there, and it was to take two years for him to clear his name.

He was finally 'de-Nazified' in April 1947 and returned to conduct the Berlin Philharmonic Orchestra – *his* Berlin Philharmonic Orchestra – the following month. Yet the smoke never completely cleared. Or, to change the metaphor, there remained many who could not get a nasty taste out of their mouths. Toscanini saw to it that Furtwängler never conducted again in America.

If one of the basic reasons why Furtwängler did not leave Nazi Germany was his illusion that he could divert some of the more unpleasant consequences of Nazi policies, the other was his rootedness in the philosophical and cultural soil of his native country, his complete and utter Germanness. This issued in a conviction of a duty of service – that the sustenance he had drawn from German soil should, through his devotion and sense of commitment, be returned to that soil and used to re-enrich it. For some the preservation of humane values in an inhumane environment could only mean emigration. For others it meant precisely the opposite. Furtwängler has as much right to be heard as any:

> I write as one who knows the Nazi regime through and through. I lived through it for twelve years. I know how many were forced to join the Party in order to survive [Furtwängler never did]. I know what dictatorship and terror mean. And I know how alien this terrible monster, nurtured in their own bosom, is and was to the

Germans, otherwise I would not have stayed there. The fact that I did stay is the best proof that there is another Germany. Let anyone who denies this wait at least until this other Germany has been given a chance to let its voice be heard again. . . . There never was a Nazi Germany – only a Germany under the heel of the Nazis.

As much in demand as ever, Furtwängler spent the few remaining years of his life in his usual hectic round of engagements. He was back in London in 1948 and conducted the traditional performance of Beethoven's Ninth Symphony at Bayreuth when the Festival was restored in 1951, and again in 1954. In October of that year he caught a chill on the journey back to his home near Montreux after recording *Die Walküre* in Vienna. Bronchial pneumonia set in, and he was taken to a clinic in the Black Forest, where, a few weeks later, on November 30, he died.

Difficult, at times remote; self-confident to the point of arrogance, yet sometimes curiously diffident; ascetic, a worshipper of nature, hater of the letter but lover of the spirit – a complex character. Few enjoyed his intimacy. He had something of the Olympian but was at the same time intensely human, with human fallibilities and unpredictabilities – a personality not unlike that of Goethe, his philosophical mentor.

He had been due to conduct at the Royal Festival Hall in January 1955. His place was taken by Sir Thomas Beecham, a friend of long standing, who addressed the audience before the concert:

> I shall not speak to you tonight about Wilhelm Furtwängler's musicianship. You know enough about that. He was a fine musician and a man of the highest integrity. In the difficult times in Germany he protected the weak and assisted the helpless. My tribute is to a man of remarkable and sterling character, and we see very few of them anywhere in these days.

The original German texts of the items in this selection are to be found in Wilhelm Furtwängler, *Vermächtnis. Nachgelassene Schriften*, 1956 (Nos 3, 7, 12, 14) and Wilhelm Furtwängler, *Ton und Wort. Aufsätze und Vorträge 1918 bis 1954*, 1982 (Nos 1, 2, 4, 5, 6, 8, 9, 10, 11, 13, 15), both copyright and published by F. A. Brockhaus, Wiesbaden.

Other sources of Furtwängler's thoughts and opinions are his diary jottings, published as *Aufzeichnungen 1924–1954*, Wiesbaden 1980 (translated by Shaun Whiteside as 'Wilhelm Furtwängler, Notebooks 1924–1954', London/New York 1989) and

Gespräche über Musik, Zürich 1948 (translated by L. J. Lawrence as 'Wilhelm Furtwängler, *Concerning Music*', London 1953). A selection of his letters was published ten years after his death (*Briefe* ed. Frank Thiess, Wiesbaden 1964). The latest biography, which reviews most of its predecessors from the first (Friedrich Herzfeld, *Wilhelm Furtwängler*, Leipzig 1941) onwards, is Hans Hubert Schönzeler, *Furtwängler*, London 1990.

The notes on the individual items at the end of the volume are intended to provide occasional background information and explanations of points of detail which may help readers to set Furtwängler's observations in sharper focus. His essays are intimately linked to their time and place, and in addition to their intrinsic value have an interest, historical and cultural, as the responses of a passionate mind to musical developments taking place around him. His style – intensely German, sometimes excruciatingly so – can be convoluted and unwieldy, and I have sometimes permitted myself the liberty of taking an Anglo-Saxon knife to particularly contorted formations. It is, after all, the meaning that counts. The core of that meaning is firm and precise, and can lay fair claim to the attention of those who enjoy the stimulating company of a great musician as he contemplates the fortunes of his art.

Ronald Taylor

Part I
The Practice of Music

1   Concert Programmes

A good concert programme, as one understands the term today, is not difficult to devise. All that is needed is a modest amount of historical knowledge, a certain regard for contemporary composers, and a kind of fashionable aesthetic label to stick on the finished product.

The label is particularly important. People today are demanding that a programme should not be just an arbitrary selection of varied items but should have a pattern to it, an individual character, with a theme or 'device' of its own, a reflection of some catch-phrase or other.

There are various such devices. One can arrange programmes on an historical basis, by epoch, for example – the pre-Classical period, the Classical period, the modern period; or by nationalities, 'schools', generations or historically demonstrable 'influences'. One can also draw on fashionable areas of comparison, such as that between pre-Classical and contemporary music. In America a well-known pianist even devised a programme in C sharp minor. It does not matter so much what the actual underlying principle is – the main thing is that it is there and that people can see from the programme what it is.

What looks attractive on paper often turns out in practice, that is, on the evening of the concert itself, to be thoroughly boring. There is a difference between the impression made by a programme on the reader and that made by the music itself on the listener. Take the common example of an evening devoted to symphonies by Haydn, Mozart and Beethoven. Someone seeing such a programme would find the combination ideal, to be subsumed under concepts such as 'stylistic unity', the 'Viennese Classics' or 'the development of the symphony'.

But what about the listener? He would feel monotony and boredom, with the works played second and third having no effect at all. In short, not a programme designed *for* the symphony but *against* it. One must realize that to absorb even one of these symphonies, despite what appears to be the relatedness of their thematic material, and with the complexities of the internal links and correlations over long stretches, makes extraordinary demands on the modern listener, attuned, as he is, to experiences of brief duration. And then three such works on a single evening, plus the apparent similarity of their idiom!

What has largely been left out of account in such one-track 'thematic' programmes, are the psychological realities that condition the activity of listening. Indeed, they *have* to be left out of account. Whatever intellectual satisfaction – slight enough, in all conscience – a thematic title may give the earnest listener, it has nothing whatsoever to do with the essence of the music itself. Music is not there in order to be perceived, reviewed or categorized in terms of historical contexts. It is there in order to be enjoyed. If a thematic programme is successful, whatever its nature, then it is in spite of the theme, not because of it. Any concept of unity cannot but be at odds with the fact that, emotionally and by its inner nature, music lives by contrasts. The law of contrasts rules equally in an individual sonata movement as in a large-scale cyclical work, in the St Matthew Passion as in a sonata by Hindemith. And it must also govern the way in which a concert programme is put together.

By contrast, of course, I do not mean a set of arbitrary permutations but what I would call 'creative contrast', where even the most marked antitheses are never completely resolved (I will not pursue this matter further at the moment, especially as, however easy it is to talk about it in theoretical terms, it embodies a law which has to be constantly observed and applied in practice).

It is therefore the primary duty of a concert programme to position each individual work in such a way as to allow it to reach its full bloom – a task considerably more humble, and at the same time considerably more difficult, than devising attractive 'thematic' programmes, even though it may offer less scope for critics to grind their axes and indulge in historical speculation.

Taking the question one step further, we can see that crucial importance attaches to the order in which the works in a particular concert are played – a consequence of music being one of the Arts of Time. With two such different works as a symphony by Haydn and a symphony by Tchaikovsky, for example, it would be impossible to play the Tchaikovsky first. The Haydn would be left sounding thin and dry, and the listener would be unable to fully appreciate its more delicate, more graceful, more precise nature after experiencing the cruder techniques used in the Tchaikovsky. *Vice versa* to follow the Haydn with the Tchaikovsky is like moving forward into the world of human problems, our modern world, so to speak. And the Tchaikovsky will never appear to better effect than when placed after such works as Haydn's.

It is therefore quite wrong to maintain, as people often do, that such and such works do not go together. It all depends on the order in which they are played, and deciding on this order is a persistent problem. There are pieces that can only be put at the end of a programme, others that can only be put at the beginning. Some undergo a radical change of nature – even a trivialization – if they are put at the end of a long programme: Beethoven's Overture Leonore No 3, for example, frequently loses its sublime quality under such circumstances and degenerates into a mere bravura exercise. The interval too can be given a specific function and serve to keep apart contrasting works which would otherwise be difficult to accommodate under one roof.

One can say, in general, that the greater the emotional and intellectual demands the composer makes, the more significant these psychological considerations become, and consequently the more difficult the arrangement of a concert programme. Such problems do not worry theoreticians or scholars in their ivory towers, for they are problems of musical reality. But as far as I am concerned, this reality is the only thing that matters, particularly as Germany today is in danger of drowning in a raging torrent of musical theories and ideologies.

At the same time there are a number of external pressures which cannot be ignored. One is the demand for contemporary works to be taken into consideration. This is both a social and an artistic demand, since music – that of the past as well – only has meaning in that it is part of life in the here and now, so that from one point of view a concern with the music of the present has a right to precede all other concerns. This must not, of course, be allowed to degenerate into a rivalry between old and new. The whole corpus of the music of the past stands before us as a living entity which is constantly changing its meaning and its relevance by virtue of the vitality throbbing through the individual works. New works have to merge with this corpus, justifying themselves at the bar not only of the present but also of the past. There is no point in a composer, or his critical supporters, trying to set up an artificial gulf between us and the past, or to diminish the past's importance in an attempt to carve out a niche for himself and avoid the issue of rivalry or comparison. The issue has to be faced. Proposals one frequently hears for keeping modern works apart from those of the past and performing them in concerts of their own must be resisted. Indeed, far from working to the detriment of a powerful modern work, the presence in the same programme of pieces by the old masters can enable it to reveal its own special significance for contemporary audiences.

Where a series of concerts is concerned, it is legitimate to raise the question of comprehensiveness. Much depends on how far such a series of concerts sets out to be representative but there are limits to what can be done. It may be possible, for example, in a season of twenty-two concerts by the Leipzig Gewandhaus Orchestra to provide a conspectus of the orchestral repertoire. But in a series of twelve subscription concerts it is more difficult, and in a series of eight the very attempt becomes ridiculous. In an eight-concert series I came across recently in one of our larger provincial cities the name of Beethoven appeared only once – and that a minor work – while the rest of the programmes were mostly taken up by second- and third-class pieces from all around the world – a sure way of provoking a crisis in our concert halls.

The fact that external considerations are taken so seriously, and this whole question of concert programmes given such prominence, only goes to show how unsure of itself the public feels at the present time. In really productive ages there was no problem about devising programmes – take the era of Beethoven, for instance, or, later, that of Liszt and Bülow. What matters is not how one plans music but how one actually *makes* it. A single satisfactory performance of a truly great work, such as a Beethoven symphony – and how rare such performances are! – constitutes a better programme than all 'thematic' programmes put together. This is the moment, the only moment, when we discover whether or not a concert has become a true experiential reality.[1] If there is anything that can be demanded of a concert programme, it is that it should ensure that great music, old or modern, should be accorded the position that is its right, *viz* should become ever more firmly anchored in the human consciousness. A musician who puts together a concert programme must see himself not as a salesman pledged to offer something to everybody, but as a guide, willing and able to express judgements and opinions. The moment he ceases to do this, and thereby fails to make what is truly great and good the centre of attraction – accepting the risk that all manner of Philistine factions will make out that such works are over-familiar, hackneyed – he performs music a disservice. Unhappily, keeping abreast of the times, however one defines this, is no longer always the same as cultivating a living music. The latter seems to me incomparably more important, more responsible – and is itself more 'abreast of the times', if the truth be told.

2 Principles of Interpretation

Our relationship to the past has become equivocal, no less in music than in all other spheres. As a result the questions surrounding the subject of how to perform the works of the past have acquired an importance which nobody had reckoned with, and the performer, the communicator of these works, finds himself bearing a crippling responsibility. The problem of interpretation has turned into a question of survival. This is a matter which requires our attention quite independently of contemporary political considerations – which, however, since they affect our everyday musical life, are also an important factor in the equation.

There are two slogans prominent in public discussion today. One is that of 'literal' performance, the other is that of 'creative interpretation'. To any normal person the former, with associated concepts such as 'adherence to the spirit of the work' and 'subordination of the performer's personality to the composer', must seem a matter of course. Every student takes it for granted that one does not contradict what the composer has written, and that it is our obligation to make our own personality take second place to the composer's intentions.

As a goal this concept of the 'literal' performance is woefully inadequate; at the most it represents the ideal of the pedant, the pedagogue, quite apart from the fact that it is simply not practicable, even in the simplest of cases. For instance, a score cannot give the slightest clue as to the intensity of a forte or a piano, or exactly how fast a tempo should be, since every forte, every fast or slow tempo has in practice to take account of such things as the size and composition of the orchestra and the characteristics of the hall in which it is playing. Moreover as far as German classical composers are concerned, the dynamics are quite deliberately not literal but symbolic, not with a precise practical meaning for each individual instrument but of a broad significance, added with the sense of the work as a whole in mind. Thus these dynamics often have to be interpreted differently for different instruments. Fortissimo for the bassoons is quite different from fortissimo for the trombones. In fact, the whole notion of 'literal interpretation' belongs rather to the sphere of literary criticism than to music, to which it is so irrelevant as to be scarcely worth discussing. The only matter of interest is how and why it has come to be seen as so important by the public at the present time.

On this subject the first thing to be said is that we appear to be dealing with a reaction. The late Romantic age of Impressionism, which has just passed, was characterized by an extreme individualism of interpretation, including the works of the past – a tendentious preference for individualistic emotionalism and vague, colouristic self-indulgence at the expense of formal structural values. Weingartner used to complain about rubato conductors, while rubato pianists still continue to dominate the scene, and are, moreover, largely to be blamed for the fact that public interest in the pianoforte and the works written for it – the wealth and beauty of which far exceed those written for any other instrument – has been steadily in decline. In the face of this it is fully understandable that there should be a concern with the composer's instructions and a demand for clarity and objectivity of performance, however inadequate a way this is, in itself, to approach the works of the great composers.

More importantly, it has never been the performers, today or in the past – the musician's confinement of his activity to one of performance is in any case not all that old – who defined the style of reproduction but the creators. This they did either indirectly, through the new challenges and new visions in their works, which also changed our perspective on the past, or directly as performers themselves. It was the creators, the composers, who provided the performer with the *raison d'être* of his activity: their very existence gave him a sense of direction and acted at the same time as a constant, if unconscious controlling influence which protected him from the most blatant of misconceptions.

All this was only possible, however, as long as composers felt themselves to be the natural heirs and consummators of the past, to which they had a living relationship. But since the 'New Music', that is to say, since contemporary composers began to see themselves as being in opposition to the 'Old Music' and thus to their own past, they inevitably lost all inner relationship to this past. They were neither willing nor able to create a style of performance for a past that no longer interested them, leaving it instead to the professional interpreter.

This was the moment when the question of interpretation raised its head and when the public somehow grasped, unconsciously, what an alarming degree of importance the interpreter had suddenly acquired. He found himself holding in his hands a treasure of incalculable value – the whole of the past – with no higher authority to which to appeal for help. This moment marked the beginning of the ludicrous overestimation of the interpreter, the performer – an overestimation to which he himself had tended from the outset, alone as a result of perpetually confronting the public. But it also marked the onset of a move to escape from his power, to restrict his influence, to lay down the path he should follow, to check his activities at every possible turn. On the one hand there emerged the view that there was no such thing as an objectively 'correct' performance but that everything was a matter of taste, and that each individual and each age had the right to refashion the past according to its own requirements. Accompanying this were slogans like 'creative interpretation' and performances 'in keeping with the spirit of the times', primitive, naive intellectualizations which did not shrink from the most palpable nonsense so long as the terms of the theory could be made to justify it.

On the other hand we had the crabbed, soul-destroying demand for 'literal' interpretations. Those propounding this view would dearly love to pronounce sentence of death on anyone who departs one iota from the composer's written text, restricting performance to exactly what is recorded and thereby reducing any subjective freedom to the smallest degree imaginable.

We can now begin to understand why it is no accident that these two apparently contrary trends in performance should make their appearance in one and the same age. There even seems to be a causal connection between them, as though they had a common origin, were like the two sides of a coin, or two streams flowing from a single spring. This common origin is in fact simply the sense of uncertainty that has taken hold of all aspects of our contemporary musical life, the sudden, enormous decline of our sure, natural instinct when confronted with the phenomenon of music in all its purity and power.

This is obviously not a situation that can last. Our relationship to ourselves – for what is our past but our own selves? – must become clearer, more vital, more fruitful and productive. We must find what is right in our dealings with the masterpieces of the past and what is wrong – what is good and what is bad. We must discover guidelines for interpretation which take us beyond the sterile worship of the literal text on the one hand and the totally vague, all-or-nothing shibboleth of 'creative interpretation' on the other.

This brings us to the heart of the problem. But first we must seek to define what it is that distinguishes the activity of the creator from that of the reproducer.

Consider the situation of the creator, the composer. He starts from nothing, from chaos, so to say. He ends with the completed work. His movement towards this goal – the task of bringing form to this chaos – is via the path of improvisation. Improvisation is the basic form of all true music. Soaring out into space, a unique entity, the work takes shape as a kind of image of a spiritual event. As an independent, organic process, this spiritual event cannot have its nature and course laid down in advance, cannot be the product of a logical programme or be conjured up by some other exercise of the human intelligence. It has its own inner logic, based on psychological laws, a logic no less compelling than any system of objective logic. In conformity with the laws of organic life every 'spiritual event' represented by a work of music carries within itself the urge towards completion, fulfilment. It is this urge, and not some arbitrary convention, that gave rise to the naturally-evolved musical forms of sonata, fugue, song-form and the rest. We might define a piece of music as 'an improvisation seeking a fulfilment' – a fulfilment expressive of its in-dwelling musical form yet remaining, at every moment and from beginning to end, improvisation.

Such is the work seen from the creator's point of view. How does it appear to its interpreter, the performer? In the first place, it is a printed source. It is not the performer's task to portray the pattern of his own spiritual life but to follow in minute detail the course of a work, long since complete, created by somebody else. He has to work backwards, as it were, not forwards, like the composer; contrary to the direction in which life evolves, he has to move from the outside to the inside, not vice versa, like the composer. His path is not one of improvisation, i.e. of natural growth, but one characterized by the painstaking assembly and arrangement of component parts. And whereas for the composer these parts, as in any organic process, merge naturally into his vision of the work as a whole, which gives them their individual life and meaning, the performer, for his part, has to laboriously reconstruct such a vision for himself out of the separate parts at his disposal. It is from such distinctions, both of the factual situation and of the challenges that flow from it, that the problems of interpretation and performance emerge.

Since it is initially the separate elements, the component parts, with which the performer has to deal, he naturally regards these as his most important data. What gave these elements life, however, the overriding vision of an artistic entity, is something to which he does not have direct access and which therefore seems to him superfluous – maybe even non-existent. (This is a far from uncommon attitude, and one that characterizes all passive and unproductive attitudes which make works of art mere objects of enjoyment.) Seen in isolation, each of these elements allows free rein to the performer's individual imagination. And indeed, whether I play a passage in this way or that, interpret a theme as lyrical rather than heroic, say, or as supple and flowing rather than tragic and ponderous, *is* a matter of taste. No court can pronounce final judgement on the issue.

A quite different situation arises, however, if one links to the individual passage what precedes and what follows it, taking within one's purview the overall context into which the composer has set his themes and motifs. When one turns one's attention to the way the piece has grown, the way one passage has evolved into another in logical sequence, and when one thus comes to see more and more of the composer's creative vision of his work *in toto*, then, and only then, will all the separate parts be seen in their true function, arranged in their proper order, with their own character and flavour. If the work as a whole is the chronicle of a 'spiritual experience', each individual moment can only receive its meaning from its position within the context of this chronicle and in accordance with the psychological laws that govern it.

It follows from this that for every musical work – and the greater, the more complex the work, the truer this is – there is only one approach, one manner of interpretation, that consistently proves to make the deepest impression, precisely because it is the 'correct' interpretation. It is worth observing, in passing, that the music of different periods and different countries lends itself in varying degrees to this conception of a work of art as the expression of a spiritual experience. We find it at its most highly developed in Germany, where individual musical forms such as fugue and sonata – also music drama, to a certain extent – are the product of just such a process of spiritual development, just such a reflection of spiritual events.

The question now arises of how the performer, with nothing at his disposal but the separate constituent elements of the work, is to proceed in order to achieve a grasp of the work as a whole. First he seeks to assemble the parts in the most satisfactory way they allow, in his judgement, arranging them as attractively as he can, rather as he would arrange flowers in a vase. But there is, of course, a vital distinction between such an arrangement of parts, however skilful, and the organic driving force which has informed the composer's act of creation. For all the performer's ability, what he achieves can never be more than an assemblage of already available, ready-made elements. Never can it match the composer's living vision of his creation, with its individual parts bonded together, as it were, by an inner logic sustained by the principle of improvisation.

No-one has described the process of re-creation, re-construction, more strikingly and more profoundly than Wagner, in the legend of how Siegfried's sword was re-forged.[1] There was no way in which even the most skilful craftsman could weld the broken pieces together. Only by grinding the fragments to dust, thus returning to the primordial state – the state of chaos, so to speak, which preceded the act of creation – can one reconstruct, recreate the work in its original form.

But how can the interpreter do this, since it is, after all, the finished work that confronts him? How, since his data consist only of individual elements, can he come to understand the work as an organic whole and the spiritual experience that underlies it?

At this point we have virtually reached the limit of what can be said on the subject. We are talking about the essence of the organic creative process, and it is extremely difficult to reach this essence through words. But this much is certain. However we define the 'totality' with which we are dealing – whether we call it form, structure, the portrayal of a spiritual experience or any other inadequate term I have used – it is only by recognizing the existence of such a totality that we can prevent ourselves from falling into a state of total chaos and confusion. So long as a work is not regarded as a stockpile of romantic

'moods', as it often was in unsophisticated circles in the nineteenth century, or as an arid mechanical exercise in abstract
forms – an equally primitive view fashionable in recent years
– but as an unfolding organism, a process of vital, organic
development, then the truth of what I have said above will
emerge of its own accord, namely, that, discounting minor
superficial variations, there is for every single work only one
approach, only one manner of performance, that is appropriate,
inherently 'correct'. This makes equally superfluous both those
ill-motivated appeals to varying species of 'personal taste' and
the facile slogan of 'faithful' or 'literal' interpretation, at the
other extreme.

All this assumes, of course, that the work in question, its
vital form and structure, is fully and properly understood, i.e.
that we are capable of 'reading' it – the real challenge facing
the interpreter and a demand made more insistently by the
present age than by any earlier age. Former generations were
unaware of the problem. Right down to the early years of
Strauss and Pfitzner, Debussy and Stravinsky, each age had its
own view of the past and its own mode of performance, so
firmly based on instinct and sustained by so much musical
conviction that, irrespective of whether it was 'right' or not, it
was fully adequate for their purposes. The structural features
of the works may have been sensed rather than understood but
in return they were less frequently ignored and distorted than
they are today.

Such knowledge has today become both more essential and
more difficult to acquire: more essential, because it is the only
way for us to retain possession of the living art of the past;
more difficult, because the present age finds itself increasingly
helpless in the face of everything governed by the principle
of organic development, while the performer, deprived of any
natural, instinctive tradition, is more and more thrown back
upon his own resources. It is thus more important than ever
before to understand the true meaning of this structural principle and to be able to fully grasp the overall vision of a work
as it emerges from its individual parts. It hardly needs to be
added that this demands a musicality which far exceeds that of
your average performer.

This is the principal source of the crisis that faces our public
musical life at this moment. It matters not that the technical
standard of our playing – particularly as a result of our contact
with America – has greatly improved, or that we are making

greater efforts than ever to raise the level of performance. Indeed, all this activity, like the innumerable theories that have been put forward on the problem of interpretation, only serves to mislead and distract attention from the heart of the matter, while revealing only too plainly the gravity and intensity of the sickness that is ravaging our musical life at the present time.

3   The Tools of the Conductor's Trade

Conducting an orchestra is an activity performed in full public view. There is no secret science of conducting, like the techniques of learning how to play an instrument, which can take a long time to master – even a whole lifetime. The public is able to observe all the mysterious messages that pass between conductor and orchestra. Indeed, conducting is just such an art of 'passing messages', whereby relatively simple movements convey rhythm, sonority, dynamics and whatever else constitutes the sound the players are required to make, down to the last little detail. The means by which this is achieved is clear for all to see. We watch the players keeping their eye on the conductor – though they frequently appear not to – and we observe the conductor's gestures. Since they are governed by the need to convey tempo and rhythm, these gestures have little scope for variation. Yet are there any greater differences that bear upon an orchestra than those conveyed by different conductors? I am not talking about interpretation, which will of necessity vary according to conductors' differing personalities, but of the physical qualities of the orchestral sound, which emerge far earlier, and often far more decisively, than anything related to interpretation.

The first question is that of the sonority itself. Why does one and the same orchestra sound full, warm, well-balanced under one conductor and harsh, brittle, jagged under another? Why – and this can be a decisive feature when the music calls for it – does an orchestra play legato under one man but not under another? In fact, does it not often seem that there is almost as much difference in sound when two different conductors conduct one and the same orchestra as there is between two different violinists, let alone two singers? There are conductors under whom the village band can play like the Vienna Philharmonic,

16

and others who can make the Vienna Philharmonic sound like the village band.

People have got into the habit of using terms like 'thought transference' and 'power of personality' to explain such things. This is nonsense. There is no such thing as a 'power of personality' which, assuming the same tempo and the same general interpretational intentions, can cause one conductor to make the shortest phrase sound smooth and coherent, like a vocal line, while under another it sounds wooden and disjointed, or even barely audible.

In reality – and we must make no bones about this – no art is more mysterious, more completely concealed than that of a real conductor. This is true not only for the public and the critics, who have to rely to a greater or lesser extent on general impressions, but also for the professionals, i.e. conductors themselves. As a young Kapellmeister, starting out on my career like scores of others, I took ages to understand why Arthur Nikisch's[1] simple movements made an orchestra sound so different, why the woodwind avoided the customary exaggerated *sforzati*, why the strings had such a resonant legato, why the brass merged naturally with the rest of the instruments and why the overall sound of the orchestra had a luxuriant warmth about it which it did not have with other conductors. I came to realize that far from being an accident, this was the consequence of the way Nikisch beat 'into' the orchestral sound, so to speak. In other words, it was not the product of his personality or his powers of suggestion (honest-to-goodness professional musicians know nothing of such things) but simply his technique.

A conductor's technique is, of course, personal and individual to the extent that it is shaped by the nature of his need to express himself. As Stravinsky, for instance, seeks a different orchestral timbre from Richard Strauss, so his conducting technique will reflect this. There is, incidentally, a technique taught universally today in textbooks – a kind of standardized skill which produces an equally standardized orchestral sound, a routine technique aimed at achieving a precise ensemble. This turns something which ought to be a matter of course into a self-justifying object of study, and a technique of this kind can never do full justice to the music. There is something dry and mechanical about it, as though the physical 'business' of conducting were oppressing the spirit of the music and threatening to stifle it. As Tolstoy once said: ninety-five per cent of all artistic activity is routine; that can be learned and is not what matters. What does matter is the remaining five per cent.

The conductor's initial task is to convey the rhythm of the music, primarily by setting the tempo, from which the precision of the ensemble and all other matters derive. This tempo is in the first place something abstract, rather as communication by radio telegraphy, using the Morse code, is abstract. The metronome indicates tempo by abstract numbers. In music, however, one is never concerned with tempo in this abstract sense but with the conveyance of reality through sound, through a kaleidoscope of melodies and harmonies and so on. If the music itself is of an abstract nature – staccato with strong accents, for example – it would be appropriate to use firm gestures that concentrated on the basic rhythm. If, on the other hand, it consists of broad, flowing melodies, such gestures would be patently out of place. In such a case the orchestra has to play each melody as a coherent phrase, i.e. as a true melody should be played, in spite of the fact that the conductor's beat can only mark the basic rhythmic structure and outlines.

This, in a nutshell, is the whole problem of the technique of orchestral conducting. How can I, the conductor, whose only ability is to wave his baton in the air, get an orchestra to play a *cantabile* theme as its nature requires, that is, as a vocal melody? In other words, how, through my gestures for conveying rhythm, can I get the orchestra to *sing*?

To a certain extent, of course, this happens automatically, in that song itself exists within a rhythmic setting, an overall rhythmic context, and the cantabile element will find expression even when the conductor concentrates exclusively on the rhythm. But this is as far as it can go, for a melodic phrase is not just a rhythmic pattern of notes, an assemblage of individual moments, but an entity which emerges, and receives its meaning, including its rhythmic meaning, from the rhythm of the work as a whole. Melody is something basically different from rhythm and at the same time – this must be understood once and for all – is of no less basic and vital a significance for the music of the Western world than rhythm.

This is where the problem of playing and listening to music – and thus of conducting it – really begins. In short, the question from which we started, the question of the conductor's technique, is, how can I get an orchestra not only to play with rhythmic precision but also to sing, with all the freedom necessary to create a vibrant vocal line? How can we unite these apparently irreconcilable opposites – technical rhythmical precision on the one hand and freedom of melodic line? Or, put the other way round: How can I get an orchestra which can sing – with those countless idiosyncracies of rhythm which can never be described and never made explicit in rehearsal but are inseparable from all music that truly sings – to play together in a manner strict to the last rhythmic detail?

Here lay the secret of the power of Arthur Nikisch, as I was able to witness for myself. Nikisch could make an orchestra sing – an extremely rare gift, let there be no doubt about that. Nor was this quality confined to comparatively straightforward contexts where the music really did consist of broad, sweeping melodies. It also extended to that infinite variety of phrases, above all in Classical music, where the unbroken vocal line – the 'melos', as Wagner called it – constantly changed its position and its pitch, moving from one orchestral part to another, often within one and the same bar. The 'melos' remains as important as ever for grasping the meaning of the work in question but its thousand different disguises make it the more difficult to recognize.

The conductor's movements that convey the rhythm, the beat, are by their nature themselves rhythmic, themselves beats, characterized by the utmost precision. But – and this is the practical problem in all conducting – this precision cannot be achieved simply through a movement in the air. What makes a group of musicians all start to play at the same time needs visual preparation. It is not the instant of the downbeat itself that produces the precision with which the orchestra enters, nor is it the precision of the conductor's gesture but the way he prepares for it. Its clarity may affect the subsequent downbeats through its characterization of the pulse as a whole but as far as the opening note of the piece is concerned – the note at which the beat is aimed – this is irrelevant. All those who conduct solely in terms of fixed points, i.e. with a strong downbeat – and ninety per cent of conductors do – are completely unaware of this.[2]

A strong downbeat has considerable disadvantages. It binds the movement of the piece to specific points, thereby restricting the natural flow of the music and reducing its expressiveness. A point remains a point, and an orchestra that is conducted in a series of points will obviously play accordingly. That is to say, the purely rhythmic substance will be conveyed with the requisite precision, while the melodic substance, everything that lies between the individual beats – which can amount to a very great deal, witness the numerous crescendos, diminuendos and other dynamics central to the music of many composers – is left totally untouched. It is characteristic of such an interpretation – and a commonplace these days – that while the rhythm and the tempo receive due attention, the music itself does not.

The power to affect a note – and this cannot be emphasized too often – lies in the preparation of the beat, not in the beat itself. We are talking about that brief, often minute instant when the beat falls, before the actual orchestral sound is produced. According to the nature of the beat and its preparation, so will be the sound that is created – precisely and absolutely so. Even the most experienced of conductors is time and again amazed to find with what incredible precision his slightest and most delicate movements are mirrored in the performance of a well-trained orchestra. This is the reason why no conductor worthy of the name can play to the audience. People used to maintain that Nikisch indulged in play-acting. I can testify from personal experience, however, and without the slightest hesitation, that any form of affectation was anathema to Nikisch, whereas a number of others who conducted 'by the book' were by no means free from affectation; with comparatively primitive attitudes towards matters of technique, they had time to think of the audience, which Nikisch would never have done, because he was concerned with musical sound and with how to create it.

Thus the conductor's power to influence the nature of the interpretation, the way in which the orchestra plays, lies entirely – we are talking of the spontaneous moment, not of rehearsals – in the preparation of the beat. Incidentally, in my view the value of rehearsals is generally overestimated. We live in an age that overrates the value of mechanical procedures. What one can teach an orchestra in the course of even the most extensive and concentrated of rehearsals is trivial in comparison to what one can achieve in a few minutes through the nature of one's beat and the instinctive, i.e. subconscious means of communication associated with it. This also explains why certain conductors – those, that is, who deserve the name and are not just stick-waggers – can, through the exercise of their individuality and their power of interpretation, coax such differing sounds from one and the same orchestra. Here too is the source of the audience's instinctive admiration for a particular conductor.

If, as I said earlier, it is the preparation, the actual beat itself, and not just its termination, that exerts the strongest influence over the sound that emerges, would it not be possible to envisage a manner of conducting which dispensed as far as possible with these terminations, these brief, fixed moments, and have recourse only to the beat and its preparation? This is no matter of mere theory. I have myself been endeavouring for years to evolve a practice of this kind. This is why many who are accustomed to the common-or-garden technique of conducting taught in our conservatoires are unable to understand my movements. They find them vague, even going so far as to accuse me of indulging in 'camouflage'. Not long ago a critic, reviewing a concert I had given with the Vienna Philharmonic, wrote as follows: 'Given the conductor's ill-defined gestures, it is beyond comprehension how the orchestra achieved such a perfect ensemble. The only solution to the mystery must be endless rehearsals.'

Not at all – that is precisely *not* the solution to the mystery. I have no more than the customary number of rehearsals and hardly concern myself at all with the technical questions of ensemble playing. On the contrary, ensemble precision is the natural consequence of my 'ill-defined' conducting. Indeed, the best proof that it is not 'ill-defined' at all is the fact that the orchestra functions with such precision. I can only repeat – there are no objective gestures as such but only those directed to a practical purpose, i.e. to the orchestra. This is the basis – the music, and only the music – on which a conductor's movements have to be judged. And it is the basis on which my gestures too are understood, as has been amply proven by the reactions of the numerous orchestras I have conducted.

Great composers are not always great conductors. But they are always great musicians and their views are of great importance for a conductor. Richard Strauss, who was more of a conductor than most composers, once said to me *à propos* a performance by Nikisch: 'Nikisch has the ability to produce a sound from an orchestra which the rest of us just do not have. I can't explain it but the fact is incontrovertible'. This is the question I have sought to address in the preceding pages, a question that seems to be particularly difficult to approach because conducting, an activity that takes place in full public gaze, is apparently expected to be accessible to the general public in its technical no less than in its other aspects. Yet experience shows that even skilled professionals, men who have made a long and close study of conducting and the issues involved in it, are reduced to silence when confronted with the phenomenon of a real conductor. If it were not so, many more of today's conductors would strive to imitate the manner exemplified in the previous generation by Arthur Nikisch.

4 Observations of a Composer

Today, in the age of theory, it is still the case that a single genuine musical 'idea', converted into actual sound, will immediately render all theories irrelevant. If, in addition, the composer possesses the strength, the determination and the discipline not only to 'have' an idea but also to carry out in the course of his piece whatever that idea requires of him, then all talk of theory becomes superfluous. And if matters were left to actual experience, that would be the end of the question.

But as things stand – and this is a highly dubious feature of our age – we have one music that is played and another that is approved, one that is performed in concert halls and opera houses and another that is discussed in periodicals and journals, one that is taken seriously in practice and another that is taken seriously in theory. Moreover this is a situation that we musicians are ourselves unfortunately compelled to take seriously.

Times have changed beyond recognition. It no longer takes courage to construct a senseless pile of sounds – 'bold experiments' is the fashionable way to describe them. But it does take courage, a great deal of courage, to write a single common chord, a single natural phrase. There used to be an unwritten law of the 'natural mode of expression', which for centuries formed the basis of all genuine music. Does that law no longer apply?

It is pointless, of course, to go on repeating things that have already been said – the mark of a generation of epigones. But equally senseless is the cult of novelty for its own sake, the encouragement of what a composer says simply because it has not been said before. We recognize that originality in a work of art resides in details, in individual moments and effects which have to be rooted in the work as a whole if they are to receive their proper meaning and their lasting validity. The most urgent question facing us is therefore not so much: How can we say new things? – a question that confronts us all the time – as: How can we create an entity, a whole?

This leads me to say a few words on the issue of tonality. Tonality manifests itself in music in two ways. In the narrow sense it connotes the relationship between a set of individual notes or harmonies, together with the particular character and flavour of that relationship. As a source of euphony, it is part of the material with which the composer works, and, like any material, subject to the process of wear and tear. That for two generations young composers have turned their backs on tonality in this sense, is wholly justifiable.

In addition to this, however, tonality has another function, a function symbolized by the cadence. The cadence is a structural element, allowing the music to acquire organic form, with a beginning, a middle and an end. In this function, as we have seen time and again, tonality is as living a force as it ever was. Indeed, it cannot die, precisely because of its quality as an organic function. Human beings, moreover, are themselves organisms, subject to the laws that govern all organic life.

If we keep this dual function of tonality in mind, we can explain the contradictory situation in which at one moment it appears old and out-of-date but at the next new and fresh – the situation where a turn of phrase leaves a tired, lifeless impression in the work of an epigone but in the hands of a master can appear like a stroke of divine inspiration. The fact that, as developments in music over the past ten years amply confirm, this distinction has not received the attention it deserves can only be due to our failure to accord sufficient importance to the principle of organic life and organic development.

A final personal observation. Music is addressed to mankind, to a public, not to a clique of so-called experts. As a composer, I cannot, in all modesty, turn my back on what seems to me the most vital consideration of all – the need to find a mode of expression that can claim general acceptance. Once this principle is renounced, the way lies open for that modern 'individualism' which is gnawing away at the roots of our music.

Part II
On Composers

5   Bach

Of all great composers, Bach, since the rediscovery of his music at the beginning of the nineteenth century, must be the one whose standing has been subject to the least fluctuation. He remains today what he has always been – the divine creator on his throne above the clouds, beyond the reach of all others.

There are a number of reasons for this. In the first place his music exudes a supreme serenity and assurance, the product of a perfect blend of melodic, rhythmic and harmonic elements which never ceases to amaze us. Even in the smallest of his pieces there is a sense of balance, a consistency in the way the individual elements are linked together, combined with a feeling of self-sufficiency and inner tranquillity characteristic of Bach's own attitude to life, giving his music a supra-personal quality.

Historians sometimes try to tell us that, set in the context of his age and compared with his contemporaries, even a giant like Bach loses the larger-than-life quality that he has for us – that he was a human among humans, one man, albeit a great one, among his many contemporaries. The truth seems to me to be quite the reverse. At no time do we become more aware of Bach's extraordinary pre-eminence, or of the difference between the works that come from his pen and those that come from the pens of others, than when one compares him with other composers of his time – with Vivaldi, for example, from whom he borrowed a great deal and many of whose pieces he adapted. Even the brilliance of Handel seems strangely arbitrary, strangely capricious compared with the serene sureness of purpose that runs through Bach's music. Concentration on the moment is linked with an immense breadth of conception, richness of detail with grandeur of overall vision. With its simultaneous view of microcosm and macrocosm, its concern both with the here-and-now and with an ultimate goal, its union of what is close at hand with what awaits us in the future, Bach's music offers us an experience of the rock-firm, unshakeable power of nature such as we find nowhere else in the annals of music.

And without our becoming fully aware of the fact, this is what makes Bach's music unique. On the one hand it is an outgoing music, direct, vibrant, insistent; at the same time it retains its self-sufficiency and autonomy, and does not betray its secrets. It eschews any attempt to stimulate or to make importunate approaches to us, while combining strength and imperturbability, tension and relaxation, pulsating life and profound tranquillity in a single unique whole.

In Bach's time certain conventions, which took the form of stylistic clichés and sequential passage-work, played a more prominent role than they did later, and Bach himself is naturally not immune to the spirit of his age. But what original qualities he brought to bear on the material that his epoch bequeathed to him! He shared with his age the monothematic principle of composition – polythematicism came with the later Classical composers – but what for these latter proved to be a limitation revealed itself to him as a profound source of inspiration.

At the same time this does impose certain limits on his music. Bach dispenses with the dynamic force of contrast, with thematic variety, giving his themes only a limited degree of individuality. Beethoven, in contrast, composes like a dramatist, creating individual themes with individually developing natures, setting them against each other like living characters which live out their lives in constant contact with each other. Bach is self-contained, so to speak, at once epic and lyrical, objective and subjective. Common to both Bach and Beethoven is the power to create an entity which is a true experience in itself, an experience which reaches its own climax and fulfilment independently of its creator.

The comparison between Bach and Beethoven is one that arises of its own accord. In Beethoven we have the great historical parallel to Bach, however different from each other the two men were. For like Bach, Beethoven does not rest until a work can stand on its own feet and follow its own path towards its culmination. He guards each work jealously lest anything should encroach upon its own unique destiny. Similarly a work by Bach ploughs its own furrow with an unerring sense of purpose like a mechanical instrument, a 'living' mechanical instrument made by nature herself. Every piece is carried to its fulfilment – or rather, finds its own way to its fulfilment – in terms of the law under whose aegis it was launched into the world. The creator of these choruses and these fugues seems to be not a human being but the spirit that rules the world, the very architect of the universe.

All the more human and vulnerable, all the more dependent on the intuition of the moment is, by comparison, Bach's great contemporary Handel, fully his equal in stature, fiery, Titanic, dazzling in his brilliance, a giant of the Baroque age – all the things that Bach was not, or was no longer, or, more precisely, had no need to be. In Bach all subjective excesses have been melted in the crucible, so to speak, and transmuted into musical objectivity, the product of a determined and irresistible urge to the creation of artistic form. So powerful is the iron grip of this objectivity that Bach's human qualities, the Herculean personality that emerges from behind the objectivity, initially pass unnoticed. He is not only the great 'objective' composer who, to a greater degree than any other, has transformed individual life into formal musical experience. To an equal extent he is the person, the creature of flesh and blood, who provides the nourishment for his works at each and every turn. As a form, a Bach fugue is the supreme manifestation of the principle of strict, logical development.

But Bach is not only the composer of taut, powerful fugues. His preludes are the products of an inexhaustible, free-ranging imagination, and the unity of the Prelude and Fugue, embodied in the *Wohltemperiertes Klavier* and in numerous organ works, is something unique to him. Subjective and objective lie side by side, free, spontaneous invention alongside strictness and discipline. The two together make up the concept of nature as a whole which is encompassed by Bach's emotional world. At countless moments in his cantatas, his Passion music, the Adagio movements of his concertos, he is the greatest subjectivist that music has ever known. So intensely did he feel Christ's suffering and redemption that in his last and greatest Passion he created a massive work comparable, in so far as the magnificent singlemindedness is concerned that dominates it from the first note to the last, only to that colossal achievement of the Romantic period, Wagner's *Tristan*. In no other works does a single ethos hold such complete sway from beginning to end, an ethos that issues from the very heart, the very soul of their creator. However far apart Bach and Wagner may otherwise be, there surges through the music of both an irresistible current of subjectivity. It is a current felt not only in the St Matthew Passion but, when one views them correctly, in more or less all of Bach's works. Embedded in every bar, every melodic and harmonic phrase, is not only the relentless principle of objectivity but also the personality of a great and unique individual. Indeed, we gradually come to realize that the one is not possible without the other, and that it is the coexistence of these opposites that constitutes the phenomenon called Bach.

It is customary to regard Beethoven as the embodiment of unfettered subjectivism and Bach as his antithesis. But in reality Bach is no more 'objective' than Beethoven, than Beethoven is more 'subjective' than Bach. It is only the means they employ, and the way they employ them, that distinguishes the two. To be sure, Beethoven works as an individual artist but the themes and melodies that he composes he develops 'objectively', assigning each to its individual role with a ruthless logic and sense of purpose. It is as though, once the themes have been stated, he no longer exercises any control over the way the piece will develop – or wishes to exert any such control. His themes are to live their own life, like the characters in a play.

Equally logical is the musical development in Bach. But here the themes are not individualized to the extent that they acquire a life of their own. It is as if the umbilical cord were not completely cut, leaving the music still attached to its creator. The point is thus not reached at which one theme is set against another in the 'productive antithesis' that sustains the music of Beethoven. But despite all the differences between them the source of their greatness lies, in both cases, in the simultaneous presence of the two extremes – the objective creative will and the subjective personality of a Titan.

This is also what the Romantics felt in Bach and what drew them to him. Since his rediscovery by Mendelssohn,[1] who remained captive to this vision throughout his life in his own oratorios and other works, they found in him their ideal composer. They saw in him their own personal saviour sent to heal their own personal sickness, the sickness of an over-sensitive ego. He could not have had the effect on the Romantics that he did if, in spite of all the differences between them, he had not struck a vital chord in them, if he had not been flesh of their flesh and blood of their blood. Seen from one angle, Bach is the greatest of the Romantics. The image that we have of him today was created by the Romantics. Subsequent ages may have broadened that image but they have not changed it.

There remains one consideration that must not be ignored. Bach was primarily a religious composer. The link between his music and the religious core of his being was so strong that it not only imposed limits on the individualization of his themes and forms but also prevented him from expressing in his music the full range of material, earthly realities, in contrast to Handel, and even more marked contrast to all later composers. This link with the highest spiritual values, which in another composer would have led to enervation, impotence, premature exhaustion, became for Bach his source of constant strength and perpetual self-renewal. It is this that makes him for us the greatest of all composers, the Homer of music, whose light still shines out across our musical firmament and whom, in a very special sense, we have never surpassed.

6 Beethoven

a) Beethoven for Today

I do not intend to speak today about the famous composer we all believe we know, the composer who has his unshakeable place in our culture, but about another composer, widely misinterpreted, largely misunderstood and much abused.

The illustrious Beethoven, the man we all claim we have in our possession, Beethoven the great Classic – has he any relevance for the youth of today as they gaze into the future? To be sure, his works are frequently enough performed and his appeal to the masses appears undiminished. Not so, however, to those more closely involved. For not only are professional musicians bored with what has become all too familiar but it almost seems as though the more modern, the more intense, the more sophisticated a person's emotions are today, the more indifferent he feels towards Beethoven's music. What is the source of this paradox?

One major difficulty with Beethoven – alongside Bach the most complete, most perfect 'pure' composer the world has seen – is that, contrary to first appearances, there are no external means of access to his music. With its roots in itself, self-contained and self-sufficient, his music is ultimately impervious to any attempt to understand it from without. Such clues to his personality as there are lead only to a vague impression of some kind of wild, uncontrollable genius. This was the way Goethe saw him, pigeon-holing him in the same mistaken way as all the others.[1] How could it be otherwise, since the simple explanation of his enigmatic character – the explanation in terms of Beethoven as composer – was one to which Goethe had no access. Instead of looking for Beethoven in his works, approaching the numerous confusing aspects of his personality from the centre, i.e. from his music, people have been trying to 'explain' his music in terms of personal characteristics and thus make it more 'intelligible'.

Thus certain prominent works such as the Fifth and Ninth Symphonies are given special attention, their vitality and inner clarity being misinterpreted as a psychological trait and then misused in order to bolster up some idiosyncratic theory or other. Desperate efforts are made to find 'links' between his life and his works. Titles, usually of slight significance, that Beethoven occasionally gave certain works or movements – 'Song of Thanksgiving to the Almighty from a Man recovering from Sickness',[2] for instance, or 'Must it be? – It must be.'[3] – are made issues of fundamental importance. Then we have the historians, carried away by the realization that contemporary with Beethoven was German Idealism, a movement with which he seemed to have a certain affinity. Kant, Schiller, Liberty, Revolution – things which are no concern of the artist *qua* artist but which were and are a ready temptation to misinterpretation.

And so it has remained. Such, for example, was Nietzsche's view – Beethoven as the untamed, childlike idealist, ignorant of the real world, blindly following his random instincts. And such is the picture presented by almost all the biographies, each with its own variations. What a contrast between these vague, indeterminate notions and the sharply defined image we have of, say, Goethe. Beethoven has been turned into a bogey-man, a larger-than-life figure whose life we find it impossible to really share. But this vision of the archetypal genius – a vision that induces ecstasy in the unsophisticated, derision in the wise and sober – is quite false.

Admittedly Beethoven led a far from disciplined life: rarely does one encounter a man who made such unqualified demands on life and followed his instincts so consistently and so completely. This is clear from the external course of his life. But how different are his works! For not only is this tempestuous Titan also the source of the profoundest, most blissful serenity, of the profoundest spiritual experience, most inspiring sense of peace and harmony that has ever been conveyed in music. In the midst of the tempest, held in the grip of a raging passion, he retains his steely control, his singularity of purpose, his unshakeable determination to shape and master his material down to the very last detail with a self-discipline unparalleled in the history of art. Never has an artist, driven by an irresistible creative force, felt so intensely the 'law' that underlies artistic creation, and submitted to it with such humility.

To what extent the modern age comprehends this situation is a moot question. The only law that the present passive and unproductive age seems to acknowledge is the law of effect, effect achieved by any means, including that of taking the public unawares. We may well ask whether this age has either the capacity or the desire to experience what requires effort on its part rather than what falls in its lap, or whether, a prisoner of its own auto-suggestion, it is prepared to grasp the significance of laws which it shamelessly chooses to flaunt.

Among those who made their position public the first, and for a long time the only man who experienced Beethoven as he really is, was Wagner. Wagner devoted a number of essays and lectures to Beethoven.[4] Some of these may strike us as overly rhetorical in parts but we must not overlook the sense of necessity that he felt to communicate his knowledge to an indifferent and disdainful public. Nor does this make his insights any the less genuine. He knew better than anyone that it was as impossible for him to talk about Beethoven as it had been for Jesus Christ to talk about faith, and it led him to conclude: 'One cannot discuss the essence of Beethoven's music other than in a mood of ecstasy.'

Of course, true as this is, both subjectively and objectively, it does not take us very far. More practical consequences flowed from a tradition of Beethoven interpretation which also originally goes back to Wagner and was carried on by Bülow. Yet at the same time anybody who knows what this tradition really means – a convenient concept for a conventional, historically-conscious conductor but totally misleading for any true musician – and how almost impossible it is to convey the 'traditional' reality of even something as modest as a single tempo marking, will not be surprised that the influence of this 'tradition' proved in the long run to be pitifully slight. Goethe's saying applies as much to the performer as to the composer: 'No-one can create something that he not already is'.[5]

One achievement will always remain to Wagner's credit. Through his writings, and even more through his performances, he was the first, investing his whole passionate nature, to reveal what Beethoven really is. He demonstrated that a merely 'correct', i.e. mediocre performance – the kind no less the norm then than it is today – is a bad performance, the more so in the case of Beethoven than of any other composer, because it ignores what lies between the lines – and it is precisely there that the essence of the music resides.

Wagner also drew attention to a vital distinction between Beethoven and other composers, a distinction that leads to the heart of Beethoven's music – the music of the mature Beethoven, that is, from roughly Opus 50 onwards.[6] This music owes far less than that of other composers to specific sensory qualities – that is to say, when working out his ideas, Beethoven does not proceed primarily from the nature of the instruments or the voices through which he conveys these ideas (the only exceptions are a handful of works such as concertos). He captures the fundamental ethos of a symphony or a quartet but rarely exploits the acoustic potential of the medium in question – the wealth of timbres achievable by the orchestra, for instance. He adapts himself to the instruments he uses but never surrenders to their power. They are vehicles for ideas that go far beyond the realm of sense perception.

Yet he is not 'abstract', as many think -- not even in his last period. Rather, it is the fiery passion within him and the determination with which he keeps his eyes on the work as a whole that prevent him from pursuing the possibilities inherent in individual instrumental and vocal situations, and from allowing himself to be carried away by these possibilities. This is why on certain occasions he will fail to exploit such possibilities, but on others will exaggerate and distort them. There are fortissimi which, though scored for ridiculously few instruments, have an inner drive and power which completely overshadow the explosive outbursts of a modern symphony orchestra. This reveals itself in performance. Confronted with the inner stresses and tensions of this music, all our genteel, refined striving after artistry and euphony proves useless. Beethoven lies beyond the limits of what people call 'Beauty'. The smouldering heat within his works consumes all who perform it, singers and instrumentalists alike. To change the metaphor – every work has to be wrenched from the consciousness of whoever performs it.

Only one thing will help the performer – the most important thing of all – namely, for him to feel his way into the structure of the work as an entity, as a living organism. With Beethoven, pure composer that he was, the structure of the work is identical with the spiritual message. This is the key to all Beethoven interpretation. But what it implies is something one cannot explain in a few words.

Wagner was the first to point to the practical implication of this organic experience of the structure of Beethoven's works. Foremost among them is the use of rubato, that almost imperceptible yet consant variation of tempo which turns a piece of music played rigidly according to the notes on the printed page into what it really is – an experience of conception and growth, of a living organic process.

This naturally demands from the performer a relentless pursuit of clarity and an unyielding self-discipline, combined with emotional intensity and infinite devotion. Today's fashionable cult of personal flair and intensity fails utterly in the face of these demands, for it has no means of access to the organic, self-contained and self-sufficient work of art. However accomplished a performer of this kind may be, he can only, when confronted by Beethoven, either behave like a headstrong 'rubato' interpreter or be led by his sense of style – as people call it – to divest himself entirely of his natural instincts and modern feelings and turn himself into a 'Classical' musician. This latter tendency is, of the two, the more dangerous and fraught with disaster, for the following reason. The powerful tensions in Beethoven's music make it necessary to observe a clarity and strictness of formal build-up, since otherwise the music would be consumed in its own flames. If the performer does not re-experience and re-live the music each time anew, these formal elements will thrust themselves into the foreground, giving an impression of regulation and prescription, of hackneyed repetition, while draining the work of its energy, the vitality of its spiritual freedom, and giving the impression that it is the 'form' that matters most. In a word, Beethoven is turned into a 'Classical' composer.

And it is this much-lauded 'Classical' Beethoven who prevails in the minds of most musicians, rules in our conservatories and dominates the performances one hears, obstructing our view of the real Beethoven, destroying him day after day. Small wonder that musicians become indifferent to him, dismiss him, or that the public become weary of him, or that the critics in our journals avoid writing about him as far as they can, or that the world in general complains about a surfeit of Beethoven.

Yet it never ceases to surprise me how obstinately loyal audiences remain to him. Can it be that the living heart of his music pierces even the densest of clouds around it?

Viewed in a wider perspective, the situation is not without its comic side when one sees the contradiction that has emerged between the journalists' view of Beethoven as the untamed genius – a view based on referring time and again to the same few egregious works – and Beethoven the mainstay of the music

industry, composer of the 'left-overs' in our concert programmes, the enemy of everything new and forward-looking.
Above all the time is ripe for us to realize that Beethoven represents for us an art of the present, an art relevant to our day
and age, not an art of the past, an historical phenomenon to
be dealt with in historical terms – in reality, that is, to be
avoided altogether.

b)   The Universality of Beethoven

During the nineteenth century Beethoven was the unchallenged king of German music. Today we may feel less inclined to accord him such a position of dominance. We have become more democratic, more concerned to see each individual figure as belonging to a group, more interested in identifying schools, influences, trends etc. than in allowing ourselves to be carried away by the greatness of individuals. In spite of this, or perhaps because of it, it may be worth raising the question of why Beethoven continues to be an exception to this tendency, why he wears a halo of unique, solitary greatness that sets him apart from the bearers of other, no less illustrious names.

What strikes one above all about Beethoven, and manifests itself to a greater extent in his music than in that of others, is what I would call the 'inner law'. More than any other composer he seeks to uncover the laws of nature, the eternal verities – hence the extraordinary clarity of his music. The simplicity that dominates his work is not that of a naive or a primitive artist, nor does it aim at achieving an immediate sensory effect, like modern popular music. Yet no music makes its approach to the listener so directly, so openly – so nakedly, one might dare to say.

We know Beethoven was anything but a swift and fluent worker and that the monumentality and simplicity of his melodies were not delivered to him ready made, so to speak. Quite the reverse. Each of his works represents the quintessence of an entire world, an entity that has been forged by his iron will from a life of utter chaos into a pattern of order, form and clarity. And this clarity, let us observe, entails renouncing all those procedures – as common in art as they are in life – for setting what one has to say in as favourable a light as possible, using formulations and emphases that make it appear more important and more profound than it actually is. The twentieth century is not poor in composers who are the very opposite of Beethoven in that they possess an extraordinary capacity for concealing, not to say obscuring, what they want to express – a feature which generally only the most simpleminded, among them a remarkably large number of intellectuals, fail to recognize for what it is.

Beethoven encompasses the whole of human nature in all its complexity. He is the universal genius. He is not primarily a melodist, like Mozart, a designer of flowing forms, like Bach, a portrayer of human drama, like Wagner. He is all these things at once, each in its own special place.

There is something quite remarkable about this. Nowhere in the whole of European music is there another composer in whom the pure-melodic and the pure-structural, the gentle and the severe, combine so perfectly in a single, living natural organism – no other music in which, to use the metaphor of the human body, flesh, bone and blood are so organically and naturally fused. The power that sweeps through this music is compelled by the inexorable force of a divine, rational will to obey the laws of organic life. It is an explosive music, ecstatic, extending the limits of human experience to their utmost, yet with no trace of extravagance or intemperance.

Such, in my view, are the principal qualities that go to make up the universality of Beethoven. Never has the world experienced a music, which, for all the vehemence of its manner, is more direct, more natural – to use the current term, more objective – than this. And because we live in an age of objectivity – in a positive sense – Beethoven has a modern relevance like that of no other composer. What nobility of emotion wells up in his most intimate of personal utterances! The most beautiful moments in his music speak of an innocence, a childlike purity, which, in spite of all their human qualities, have an otherworldly aura about them. No composer has ever understood more about the harmony of the spheres or the inner peace of the Godhead. And it was from him that the words for Schiller's *Ode to Joy*, 'Brothers, there must be a loving Father living above the starry firmament!,'[1] received their true, living meaning, a meaning that lies far beyond the reach of words.

In the soul of Beethoven the musician there lies something of the soul of the innocent child. He is totally without that emotionalism and sentimentality that come from an inward-looking concentration on self. If Beethoven is emotional, then it is the emotionality of nature, as manifest in the elemental power that emanates from the heart of the universe. He never sets out to sing praises or to pay homage, nor does he set out to give the impression of being profound. Indeed, he is not concerned to give any impression at all. He just *is*. That is the source of his real profundity, of his true innocence.

c)   Beethoven and Us. On the First Movement of Beethoven's Fifth Symphony

By 'us' I mean the man in the street not the musician, the composer. The interests of the two do not necessarily coincide. This is mainly because the composer is tied to a particular body of raw material – or, more accurately, because his material (modern harmony, rhythm etc.) is at a particular stage in its historical development which imposes strict limits on his activity. From the contemporary composer's point of view Beethoven's is a distant world, and although certain individual features of his language, such as an emphasis on structure and the conciseness of his musical argument, may still have some-thing to teach the present age, modern composers in general are indifferent to Beethoven and his problems.

But the man in the street feels differently. According to the historical view modern culture – in our case modern music – is an appropriate expression of the age only by virtue of the fact that it is there. But because modern composers are so dependent on the state of their material – some might say, are so much at its mercy – the question arises, to what extent are they capable of giving full and free expression to the spirit of the age?

There is a widely held theory that European music has vir-tually come to an end, and there are people prepared to defend this declaration as passionately as if it were an article of religious faith. However understandable it may be in human terms to generalize from one's own shortcomings and thereby make them appear not to be confined to oneself; and however willing we may be to concede that, to judge from their own activity, the proponents of such a theory may be perilously close to confirm-ing that music has indeed come to an end – we must not underestimate the dangers inherent in such attitudes or fail to recognize the manifold signs of a serious crisis in our musical life. What does the situation look like if we direct our attention, not to the controversial and dubious works being produced at the present time but at music like Beethoven's, which has continuously demonstrated its vitality over the past hundred-and-fifty years?

Let us turn now to Beethoven's Fifth Symphony. I do not propose to offer what people call an 'historical assessment' of the work. Its genesis, its status are not the subject of these remarks. What does interest me, however, is to examine, on the basis of this symphony, the ways in which we react today to certain musical facts. In the face of all the irresponsible, flowery nonsense about music being bandied around today it is essential that we keep our eyes firmly fixed on the task in hand. I shall endeavour to talk as little as possible about emotions – including my own – and to concentrate as far as possible on facts derived from Beethoven's own score.

The opening of Beethoven's Fifth Symphony is no usual opening. On the contrary, it is unique in the history of music. We are not facing a first subject in the conventional sense but four bars serving as a kind of motto inscribed at the head of the movement in capital letters. The well-known phrase attributed to Beethoven about 'fate knocking at the door' makes the point:

When we look closely at these opening bars, we find that what appears to be two symmetrical periods, each of two bars, is irregularly notated, in that in the second period the final note is held over two bars instead of one. Since this cannot be put down to mere chance – the same notation is found everywhere in the movement where these bars are repeated in their entirety – one has to ask oneself what lies behind it. For it must have a reason. Felix Weingartner,[1] a conductor who studied Beethoven's symphonies in great depth, went into the question of this extra bar in his book *Hints on the Performance of Classical Symphonies*, and evolved a detailed theory which revised the phraseology of the entire first movement on the basis of this extra bar. It is unnecessary to enter into a discussion of Weingartner's theory – it is completely false – but it does make one wonder how it is that so experienced and knowledgeable a conductor could fail to recognize at once the obvious reason behind Beethoven's notation.

At all events the question cannot be answered by reinterpreting the phraseology of the whole first movement for the dubious satisfaction of demonstrating that this superfluous bar is in fact not superfluous at all. But there is another, particularly interesting aspect of the problem. From the original score, which has recently been published in facsimile and thus become readily accessible, we can clearly see that Beethoven added this disputed bar only after the first movement was already engraved in full score. So important did this bar appear to him that he inserted it at every corresponding point in the movement, that is, at the beginning of the recapitulation and at the end.

What led him to do this? The question is easily answered. Simply to indicate that the second pause was to be held longer than the first. And to what end? Surely in order to make the listener aware that these four bars, with the two pauses, form a self-contained unit which is to be separated from the rest of the work. In other words, the extension is structural in purpose.

As I said, these four bars are in the nature of a motto, a chapter-heading, at the opening of the symphony. Only then does the work proper begin. The further the work progresses, the clearer the function of the four bars becomes, until at the end they emerge as the dominant idea of the entire movement. Maybe Beethoven himself only became aware of the situation as his work proceeded, and subsequently felt the need to make the notation reveal what was at stake – hence the extension of the second pause. This is all there is to the question over which Weingartner and many others racked their brains in vain.

What conclusion should we draw, for our part, from the procedure that Beethoven adopted? First, if it comes to deciding between whether a piece of music is properly laid out and notated, and whether it 'sounds' right, Beethoven puts the sound first. For him music is primarily something listened to, not something thought out. This is an important point for us musicians today. For Beethoven what mattered above all was the process of listening as an immediate, biologically-conditioned experience. Music that was not heard, however 'correct' it might be, simply did not exist as far as he was concerned. In his eyes a grasp of the formal structure of a work was an absolute precondition for a grasp of the meaning of that work as a whole, and as these opening bars of the Fifth Symphony show, clarity of structure was among his first and unconditional demands. That meant that it was not sufficient for the structure just to be latent in a work as it stood – which it was anyway in the whole of European music at Beethoven's time; it had to be directly felt and heard, had to get under one's skin, so to speak.

As far as the first movement of Beethoven's Fifth Symphony is concerned, therefore, it would be disastrous if the listener did not instantly grasp the function of the first four bars. It is a process analogous to that of understanding the sense of a logical arrangement of words. Beethoven's music demands to be understood as a logical utterance, in the same way as a lecture or a sermon consisting of words and concepts.

Many people might assume that this is a matter of course. Far from it. To be sure, the demand that musical works be clearly and logically constructed has always been heard, more loudly at certain times than at others. But it has never been taken as a matter of course. And today it certainly is not. It seems to me important for us to realize how different Beethoven's conception of music is from that held by many contemporary composers. So-called atonal music, of course, is based on other principles but today's tonal composers too have long since abandoned the requirement, as understood and laid down by Beethoven, that there should be a logical consistency about a piece of music. To what extent are we able, and entitled, to revive this requirement in and for our own age?

Let us return to Beethoven's score and see how the opening theme develops. First there are two four-bar periods which firmly establish the principal key of C minor; these four-bar periods then give way to two-bar periods which intensify the pace and drive it urgently on towards a new point of rest, a new fermata, held by the first violins alone. This fresh pause does not have the monumental character of those in the opening bars but is rather like a dam against which the passionate raging flood of the preceding bars dashes itself and expends its energy. Wagner said it should be sustained 'for a long time and with trepidation':[2]

The opening motif, heard once instead of twice, then moves suddenly into the subdominant, and there follows a similar pattern – two four-bar periods are compressed into two two-bar periods. Then comes a remarkable development. The two-bar periods are compressed further into one-bar periods, the melodic configuration of this single bar taking over what had formerly covered two bars, and this one bar is repeated six times, a tone higher each time, until it finally arrives at the upper C:

The intensification builds up at a hectic pace. Once the upper C minor has been reached, a massive tutti breaks loose in two expansive four-bar periods which lead, at their climax, to a dramatic change of direction with the sudden violent invasion of the diminished seventh chord, which wrenches us out of the world of C minor into that of E flat, the relative major, the key of the second subject:

One has the feeling that the whole movement is turning on its mighty axis at this point, pivoting to face the arrival of a fresh subject.

It is clear that in what I have sought to describe here the disposition of the periods plays an important part. A considerable part of the musical action lies in the metamorphosis of four-bar periods into two-bar periods, and from two-bar periods into single bars. This is what takes place in the foreground, so to speak. But there is also another kind of periodization, one that concerns not the *kinesis* of the work but the *stasis*. It is what Weingartner appealed to in his attempt to explain the extra bar at the beginning, i.e. the periodization of the movement as a whole, or, more accurately, the division of the movement into regular sections generally of two or four bars. It is a periodization that underlay the whole of music in Beethoven's time, and was taken for granted by Bach as by Mozart. Haydn, and, under his influence, Beethoven, deviate more frequently from the norm but such deviations are to be seen only as exceptions to a basically unchallenged rule. Today, when this principle has ceased to apply – I am thinking in particular of the irregular rhythms and ostinato figures in the works of Bartók and Stravinsky[3] and their followers – we are beginning to question its purpose and value.

Contemporary composers avoid regular periodization precisely because they find it too regular. Changing rhythms are considered to be richer, more vital, closer to life than music divided into symmetrical periods. But the fact is overlooked that symmetry permits far richer and more subtle relationships between the various individual parts of a piece of music than do periods of irregular length. A piece with irregular rhythms is rather like an area of wild countryside with no paths or landmarks. One manages to fight one's way through it but never knows where one is. A piece that has periods of the old kind, on the other hand, with associated features such as key relationships and the tensions inherent in the patterns of Classical cadences, is like a region in which lines of communication run in every direction and where there are fast and unambiguous ways of getting from one point to another. The 'periodization' of a region like this is such that one knows at any time and in any place exactly where one is or exactly where one is going.

This is not just idle knowledge. It reflects a fundamental biological need of all creation. The periodization of music was not just a matter of intellectual concern, a way of helping people to understand a piece, but something that corresponded to a basic, elemental need felt throughout the whole of existence. The modern view that non-periodized music, with its irrational rhythms, was a feature of an earlier, more natural phase of musical thought and feeling has nothing to commend it. Historically, irregular, irrational rhythms have always been countered by the strict periodization of *ratio*. Put another way: behind irregular rhythms lies the euphoric spirit of freedom that scorns the discipline of structure, whereas rational structure aims at the creation of form, which seeks to absorb and give expression to all the forces of life, including those of freedom and irrationality.

Nietzsche coined the terms Apollonian and Dionysian to characterize the dichotomy.[4] In our present context, however, we need to realize that we are not dealing with forces that are bound to be in conflict with each other but with the challenge to reconcile them, the challenge taken up by Beethoven. I shall return to this issue later.

Let us go back to our starting-point, the first movement of Beethoven's Fifth Symphony. I have already pointed out that it is the changing periodization that constitutes the 'action' of the movement, the foreground, so to say. On the broader front the movement can then be divided into larger regular periods and groups of periods which give scope for further correlations and analogies, making up the background. This background provides the network of links between the parts. Thus each time a theme reappears, whether in the middle of a movement or at the end, its nature has changed, because it now bears with it further associations of the past and presents itself in a new light. The entire logical build-up of the first movement of the Fifth Symphony is only possible because this background is constantly and uninterruptedly present in the listener's mind throughout the piece. It is this background which gives all Beethoven's works, whose foreground seems dominated by violent outbursts and eruptions, their coherence and shrouds them in an atmosphere of peace and serenity. Underpinning the structure as a whole, it allows the emotional intensity to build up into climaxes, while at the same time acknowledging the interplay between tension and relaxation that is an inherent feature of all existence. A work by Beethoven is thus a simultaneous presentation of a foreground of spontaneous action and a superordinate background, a nexus of correspondences and relationships from which the foreground derives its freedom of action and its meaning.

An observation *en passant*. I have referred a greal deal to periodization in music, specifically Beethoven's music, perhaps implying that nothing else is at stake. To be sure, the structural aspect is of fundamental importance, particularly in so-called 'absolute' music, and one will never get to the heart of this music if one does not make structure one's point of departure. At the same time the structural web of abstract tensions and relaxations by no means constitutes the whole content of this music, for these tensions are human in origin and presented as objects for human experience.

In the nineteenth century the appreciation of music, largely drawn from the experience of Beethoven's works, was basically a reflection of the listener's emotions. Objective musical events, i.e. the works themselves, became equated with our subjective responses to them, the latter being regarded as what mattered most. Such an attitude leads nowhere, since it focuses on the subjective self rather than on the music.

This is by no means to imply that music, and in particular Beethoven's music, is incapable of expressing human emotions, or does not seek to do so. Quite the reverse. There cannot be any doubt that Beethoven did not just create abstract structures but that he filled his music with the tensions generated by his own emotions as a human being. Joy, sorrow, reverence – these and many subtle variations of them which we cannot encompass in words but which find firm, precise expression in music, all infuse his works.

To bring these emotions into the discussion here has nothing to do with the 'Romantic' interpretations of the nineteenth century which are now totally played out. At the same time there are composers – Stravinsky is one of them – who deny that music is capable of expressing emotions at all. Here I will say only that composers as different as Beethoven and Stravinsky naturally proceed from different starting-points. Far be it from me to call Stravinsky's starting-point illusory and unreal – after all, Stravinsky is a real composer and has had a decisive influence on the music of our time. But by the same token neither can I accept Stravinsky's peremptory claim that Beethoven's starting-point was illusory and unreal. The living reality of Beethoven's music and of the influence it has exerted over the past hundred-and-fifty years or more is not a matter that will be decided by the opinion of one man, even if that man be Stravinsky.

Let us return to Beethoven's score. The second subject of the first movement of the Fifth Symphony, to which we should now turn, falls into two contrasting parts. The first part is an extended form of the opening motif, played by horns alone; the second contains the second subject proper:

I remember a remark once made to me by Richard Strauss. We were walking together in the mountains and talking about second subjects, in particular those of his own works, when one of us mentioned that of the first movement of the Fifth Symphony. 'Nothing like that has ever been written since!' Strauss exclaimed. 'Nobody else has concentrated so much gentleness and power, such confidence and clarity of expression into such a tiny space!' I have never forgotten these words, coming, as they did, from a man otherwise so taciturn and unemotional.

The four bars of the second subject, a moment of idyllic calm resting on the six-four chord, are repeated three times. There follows a gradual build-up to the diminished seventh chord heard earlier, and an onwards surge over ten bars towards a third theme, based on a two-bar cadence-like motif:

At first glance this looks like a conventional closing passage. But on closer inspection we see that the significance of this third theme emerges from the position it occupies, the way it is illuminated by the fortissimo that Beethoven prescribes at this point – a dynamic marking he uses very sparingly. So what looks initially like an ordinary, almost commonplace passage acquires a profound significance, transporting the listener from a gentle valley to a radiant mountain-top, from a mood of serene contemplation to one of glowing virility and vigour. So overwhelming is the intoxication of the moment that it takes sixteen bars, in E flat major, for the feeling of exaltation to subside.

Talking about music without having the score constantly in front of one's eyes, and the sound of it in one's head, is an unsatisfactory business. But if we review the whole of the first section of this first movement of the Fifth Symphony, we cannot fail to observe how naturally the music unfolds in spite of the heterogeneity of its component parts. Rarely do we encounter one, two, even three subjects which are so fundamentally different, drawn from such different realms. Yet at the same time they complement each other as though they had been composed with each other in mind. Let us be clear on this point. There is nothing surprising about finding such contrasts in Beethoven – since Haydn contrast had been one of the principal means of advancing the action in all genres of absolute music. What does amaze us is how these contrasts combine to form an organic whole. Neither the first, nor the second, nor the third subject is exceptional in itself. Exceptional is the way all three combine in a process of symbiosis.

On closer inspection we become aware that what is responsible for this is above all the way in which one theme emerges from the other. Each individual bar that the listener experiences carries within itself something of every preceding bar in the movement, from the very first bar onwards. Slowly but unwaveringly the music reaches out into the realm of temporal experience – music being an art of time, in the Greek division of the arts – leading the listener from one point to the next. He cannot follow any other path than that which the composer has laid down; he feels at every moment that what comes was bound to come, and in the way that it came.

Thus the way in which the various elements combine must necessarily be bound to the order in which they make their appearance, and this order in turn results from the way each individual element is made to grow emotionally out of its predecessor. This gives the music a quality of inevitability, as though it were unfolding independently of its creator. Such music is often described as 'dramatic', the themes developing through interaction with each other like the characters in a play. It is the relentlessness with which this takes place, a kind of refusal on Beethoven's part to intervene in the self-generating creative process, that constitutes the uniqueness of his *modus operandi*, so different from that of Mozart, the divine bearer of melody, or of Bach, the supreme lyricist – compared with Beethoven – to say nothing of others.

Moving as Beethoven's music can be, it is never self-indulgent, never wallows in its own emotions. There are those who say that Beethoven's powers of melodic invention were limited, and they draw a comparison with the endless stream of melodies that flowed from the pen of, say, Bellini. But the reason Beethoven did not write melodies like Bellini is not that he was unable to do so but that his mind embraced all the richness and complexity of the world – and the world does not consist just of melodies. To a greater degree than any other composer, not excluding Mozart and Bach, he assigned each melody, each motif, each subject its individual place. The masculine and the feminine, the strong-willed and the gentle, the tiniest detail and the all-embracing panorama – everything comes together to form a harmonious unity that defies understanding. Beethoven is the great 'lawgiver' of music. His work is not dominated by melody, like Mozart's and Schubert's, or by counterpoint, like Bach's, or by sensuous harmony, like Wagner's; it is not governed by drama and passion, let alone by irony. All these forces are fused together, as in an alloy, and this fusion seems in some extraordinary way to acquire a higher degree of naturalness through the formative process.

In sum, it is as though an uncontrollable torrent has been subdued and deliberately channelled in a chosen direction. Infinite power has been forced into finite forms. It confronts us as a paradox, even as a kind of miracle. After all, infinite content and finite form are contradictory concepts, especially if that content has an absoluteness and a dynamism that burst any restrictions laid upon them.

This strikes at the very heart of the matter, the essence of Beethoven's creative genius. It is an essence captured in a couplet of Goethe's:[5]

> *Und keine Zeit und keine Macht zerstückelt*
> *Geprägte Form, die lebend sich entwickelt.*

> (No time, no power can destroy
> created form in its living development)

If we ask what elements go to make up this 'created form' – in the case of the first movement of the Fifth Symphony, what associations, allusions and emotions coalesce, then culminate in a single ecstatic chord – I must admit that there is no answer we can give. We experience this form as a reality but are unable to explain how and why the individual parts combine to produce an integrated work of such formidable power. Yet what we cannot fail to notice – and what Goethe clearly meant – is how homogeneous, 'simple' the artistic utterance ultimately is. A situation of the utmost complexity is expressed in a form that is simple by comparison. In times when traditions were still strong – in the age of Bach and Mozart, say – simplicity of expression was more or less taken for granted. Nobody was aware of a problem. But for Beethoven it *was* a problem – which is what, as I see it, gives him a special place in the history of music. For later composers simplicity of expression has by no means been a desirable goal in the way it was for Beethoven throughout his career (there is, incidentally, nothing intrinsically complex about the so-called late Beethoven – the complexity exists only for those who cannot grasp the inner associations).

Part of the explanation for this lies in Beethoven's personality, which was a strange mixture of unruly, unbridled passion and a longing for lucidity and harmony. A leading graphologist once told me that Beethoven's handwriting revealed a violent temper which was beyond his power to control. From one angle this may be so. But as a musician, I can only counter by asking where, among the millions in the world, can one find a man who more perfectly exemplifies through the living reality of his music the power of self-control that issues in the victory of that lucidity and harmony?

Moreover to a greater degree than almost any other composer Beethoven derived his music from exclusively musical data. He thus felt the obligation more strongly than others to think his musical ideas through to the end – ideas which never came from without but always evolved in their own terms. And this he also did in his own terms. This process of thinking an idea through to the end ultimately means no more and no less than reducing it to its simplest form, its basic formula.

We are better informed about Beethoven's methods of working than about those of many of the other great composers. We know that it was his habit to enter the various stages in the emergence of his works in sketch-books, a number of which have survived. These sketch-books are one of the richest sources of information we know. They reveal, for instance – to our amazement – that some of the happiest, simplest, most exciting parts of his works are those that cost him the greatest effort. It is a quite different situation from that found in Bach and Mozart, into whose minds music surged in a mighty flood, collecting in the pools and wells of their imagination. Beethoven's progress was laborious, unpredictable, explosive and followed the path that led from confusion to order and clarity. The themes and ideas that fill his sketch-books are initially complex and become progressively simpler. His aim was clearly to find the simplest way of formulating his thoughts, the 'created form' of which Goethe wrote. A simplicity of this kind is no everyday phenomenon. It has what one might be tempted to call the power of redemption.

For anybody who does not understand what is at stake the path from complexity to simplicity may look like the path from wealth to voluntary poverty. And whoever fails to understand the meaning of the process of liberation and purification to which Goethe's couplet points[6] will fail to recognize the blessings that this simplicity has brought. Many modern composers are wholehearted believers in complexity for its own sake. Intellectual constructs like the twelve-tone system are only possible in an age which has turned its back on the profounder sense of simplicity, an age that worships the intellect and invests complexity with an almost religious significance. It is like comparing the complexity of a modern machine, say an automobile, with the simplicity of a living creature, a living body, be it animal or human. When we look more closely at the way its parts combine, it becomes obvious that a living body is infinitely more subtle, more universal than any mechanical contrivance invented by man ever can be. It should be precisely those who are imprisoned in the confines of their own thoughts, caught up in the intellectual web of their rigidly materialist attitudes, who should feel the simplicity of Goethe's 'created form' as a liberation from the confinement of the individual ego. Or perhaps the reverse is the case – perhaps such a liberation is what they most fear.

Certainly the simplicity characteristic of earlier ages – the simplicity of Mozart, for example – may often appear to us today like the innocence of Paradise before the Fall, and to surrender unconditionally to its attractions may smack of escapism, a romantic flight from reality. But Beethoven's simplicity is something different. It is of immediate concern to us, and I have not the slightest qualms about maintaining that his central importance for us today is inseparably linked to his unwavering pursuit of this simplicity.

It has not yet been sufficiently realized that at the heart of Goethe's phrase 'created form in its living development' there lies a special problem for us today. What we here perceive on the sublime level of Beethoven's music is something found equally at lower levels throughout the whole of music in the last few centuries. One might even say that every song in an operetta, every popular tune of the moment – short as its life may be – has in it something of this enigmatic quality of 'created form'. It shines through the songs of Schubert, it is found at certain moments in Wagner and occurs in a host of other different shapes and guises. But as to all the things that go to make up this situation, the composer himself knows nothing. All the more conscious do we become of what is at stake when we subsequently set out to follow his creative processes. Indeed, it is often possible to say that the simpler and more direct the outcome, the more involved and complex the preceding stages. Even for a popular song to achieve its effect one needs a concept of the 'masses', of a collective unconscious, by virtue of which the song suddenly makes people feel that they are members one of another. This group consciousness also permeates the supreme manifestations of 'created form', such as the symphonies of Beethoven, and directs the great artist in his search for simplicity and definitiveness of expression.

We may even go so far as to say that the will to simplicity is synonymous with the strength to achieve it, the strength to rediscover one's identity in art. This needs to be said here because especially in recent times there have been trends in our artistic life which allow no scope for 'created form' in Goethe's sense. The theory and practice of Schoenberg's twelve-tone system, for instance, which has attracted an increasing number of followers over recent years, has no place for the concept, and the philosophy of music that underlies it is wholly and utterly distinct from that which underlies all music that went before, including Beethoven's. Whatever view one has of twelve-tone music, one is bound to take account of this fundamental distinction.

Our contemporary situation is, of course, different from Beethoven's. We do not live in his age and cannot employ his artistic means. Nevertheless to concern oneself with Beethoven's music is a process that leads us back to our own selves. It is not just that certain of his techniques, such as his emphasis on structural considerations, still have a relevance for us today. Over and above this there is in the intensity of his struggle to master his material in the name of simplicity, of 'created form', something that touches a raw nerve in our body. For whatever the ways in which it expresses itself, the urge to compress a message of infinite power into a framework of finite parameters, the impulse to achieve simplicity of expression, are pressures that have by no means completely disappeared from our society. But if we were to cease to express ourselves in symbolic terms, i.e. directly and simply, and to fail to recognize ourselves any more through symbols, we would lose our sense of art as we have always understood the term.

Returning now to the first movement of the Fifth Symphony, I wish only to draw attention to its most significant remaining features. The development section is characterized by the same extraordinary terseness that dominates the rest of the movement. Normally the return of the opening section after the development, the so-called recapitulation, is a key moment in works in sonata form, but here things are different. Far from being prepared and introduced, the recapitulation, led by the motto theme, is suddenly there. The reason behind this abnormality only becomes clear after we have heard the movement through to the end and fully understood the function of the motto theme in the movement as a whole. Indeed, such is the dominance of this theme that its exploitation can be said to constitute the conceptual principle of the movement as a whole.

Nor is the recapitulation itself a mere repetition. The psychological situation has changed. The first subject is now reflective, lyrical in character, and the great menacing pause of the exposition has been turned into a cadence of lamentation, given to the oboe; all the more powerful, in consequence, the way in which the movement then regains its momentum.

It may well have been the exceptional tautness of the movement, consisting, as it seems to do, entirely of muscle and sinew, that aroused in Beethoven the feeling that he needed an extended coda. Haydn and Mozart attached little importance to the coda – the section which brings the sonata movement to a conclusion after the action proper, carried by exposition, development and recapitulation, is at an end. Beethoven, however, makes it the occasion to allow his themes to desport themselves at will, pursuing to the very end the implications of his initial vision. There is a point where the opening motto theme reappears, this time without the fermata, combined with an upward surge of all the violins in unison – the last time the fearful world of the opening is conjured up:

Weingartner wrote of these bars:

> I know of no passage in the whole literature of orchestral music
> that makes such a powerful impact, despite the fact that there are
> no more instruments playing than in a Haydn symphony. It is as
> though these string and woodwind players were giants! Is the power
> of the thought so great that our spiritual ear hears more than our
> physical ear?

Beethoven drives the music onwards and upwards with
remorseless intensity, as though in a trance, until the gigantic
opening figure, now magnified to fearful proportions, reappears
for the very last time. Then a few brief bars of reminiscence,
pianissimo, like a distant dream, and an abrupt, emphatic conclusion. So, after a span of little more than ten minutes, a
tragedy by Shakespeare or Aeschylus has been played out, using
the gestures and language of music.

Looking back on the movement as a whole, after having
absorbed all the individual parts of which it is made up, we are
particularly struck by its intensity and by the homogeneity of
the final impression it leaves. Then Beethoven's ceaselessly
creative mind immediately transports us from the titanic world
of this movement into the spiritual peace, punctuated with
moments of heroic grandeur, of the second. Then follows the
Scherzo, with its glances back to the world of the first movement, leaving the symphony to culminate in the Finale, a movement the like of which nobody but Beethoven would have dared
even to contemplate. Here once again we find ourselves confronting that characteristic of Beethoven's that we mentioned
earlier – his way of proceeding from totally different sources of
inspiration towards an ultimate unity. One thought grows out
of another – that is to say, the sequence of his thoughts is the
determining factor. Only in this order could they come together
to form the work as it lies before us. Beethoven did not compose
an idea: the idea developed of its own accord from the musical
material on and with which he was working. Only in this way
has it been possible for the 'ideas' in his works to acquire the
immense suggestive power that they have exercised from the
very moment of their creation.

Time and again one comes across people who feel they have
to distance themselves from Beethoven on the pretext that his
work is sometimes 'literary' in content, like Liszt's Faust Symphony, or like the symphonic poems of many later composers,
based on the pattern of *lamento e trionfo*, 'from darkness to light',

in their works.[7] But such notions were totally alien to Beethoven. His manner of composition was objective, functional, devoid of all pretension. It was not in his nature to say anything in other than the simplest form – the product of thinking his musical thoughts through to the end, as I described it earlier. His ability to do this, with a power unique in the history of music, is the ultimate source of his towering authority.

Finally a few general observations. The musical means that Beethoven employed are those of his age. His melodic, harmonic and rhythmic material hardly differs from that used by his predecessors Haydn and Mozart. Indeed, one might even say that Mozart made fuller, more flexible, more sensitive use of his resources, and that as far as harmony and counterpoint are concerned, Bach was more consistent, more rigorous, more 'progressive', as people call it. Yet we can still feel today that, at the profoundest of levels, the revolutionary power that issues from Beethoven's Fifth Symphony has by no means exhausted itself. In the presence of this music those of us who are still capable of spontaneous thought and emotion forget all that so-called historical awareness which we men of the twentieth century drag around with us like a lead weight. Beethoven forces himself into our consciousness in the way Goethe once said of Byron – 'not in Classical or Romantic garb but like a man of the present day'.[8] One-hundred-and-fifty years on we still cannot resist seeking an objective explanation for the extraordinary effect he creates.

I should also like to draw attention to what seems to me another important question – that of the relationship between Beethoven and his listener. If something is 'not quite right' in the relationship between an individual and society – as is typically the case where the artist and his public are concerned – one must first seek the reason and try to establish whose 'fault' it is, as people tend to put it. It may rest with the inability of the public to rise to the flights of the artist's imagination; on the other hand it may lie with the artist, who has failed to make his message clear. In either case it is for the artist himself to decide which it is. Beethoven always seeks the fault in himself. It is precisely this, it seems to me, that demonstrates his ceaseless striving for directness and clarity.

Goethe once said: 'If a person expects me to listen to his opinion, he must express himself clearly. I have enough uncertainties of my own'.[9] It is a remark that puts one in mind of Beethoven. One can make direct psychological deductions from an artist's style about his relationship to his public – that is, to the kind of public he seeks and courts. Beethoven takes his public seriously, extremely seriously. He is not out to sermonize or to overwhelm them, let alone to browbeat them into submission by one or other of the means that have become so fashionable in recent times. Any such methods he would indignantly reject. His insistence on a strictly logical pattern of musical argument in which there can be no break, even for a single moment, shows how he sees his relationship to his listeners, whom he sets out to convince and by whom he wishes to be properly understood – a relationship based on a communion of minds. They are his partners, his equals. Not only does he take them seriously, as seriously as he takes himself – he sees them as his neighbours, whom it is his responsibility, as the Bible says, to love as himself. He both assumes the presence of an audience of equals and helps to create such an audience. Indeed, his music is virtually responsible for the creation of the modern concert-going public and for the development of musical life as we know it. With each performance there comes into existence a kind of ideal community.

In Beethoven the Dionysian and the Apolline, ecstatic abandon and cool sobriety, find common cause. He sweeps us off our feet by his powers of persuasion. He cannot contemplate a musical utterance that is not brought to a balanced, unequivocal conclusion; but nor can he contemplate one that confines itself to the intellectual realm, to a smug satisfaction with a skilful technical achievement.

And for all the mysterious power that he exerts over us, he does not crave this power. He had no wish to lord it over us, like many modern composers who affect an attitude of splendid isolation, nor does he seek to set himself apart from the rest of society. He is not a Romantic – he does not indulge in irrational outbursts, or lose his self-control, or bask in the glory of his own achievements. And above all, he never intimidates us.

This is perhaps the consideration from which Beethoven's message draws its greatest relevance for us today. It has become increasingly evident that the crisis in which we find ourselves at the present time – in politics and culture in general no less than specifically in music – is in the truest sense a crisis of society. Groups and sects have emerged which take a perverse pride in considering themselves totally irreconcilable with the rest of society. Ridiculous as it may sound, the only relationship between the musical avant-garde of music and those who were brought up in an earlier tradition appears to be one of mutual intimidation and destruction. We seem to have abandoned the belief – an unquestioned assumption in any sound, healthy age and the basis of any genuine culture – in the infinite variety and inexhaustibility of the living manifestations of nature. There are many roads to Rome, as the proverb has it, but today everybody seems only to know the particular road to which, for whatever reason, he has decided to commit himself.

Small wonder, therefore, that the intimidation formerly practised in certain quarters – and still being energetically pursued in those quarters today – should have provoked the Nazi state at that time to reply with its own form of intimidation, namely with its proscription of what it called 'degenerate art'.

In the way he creates his music, the way he communicates with us in his music, Beethoven eschews intimidation and coercion of any kind. Coercion shows itself only when other means have failed; and only a society that no longer believes in the power of the mind to make its own decisions is prepared to accept the decisions imposed upon it by an authoritarian state. Beethoven makes his own decisions – not in an authoritarian manner but in such a way as to allow everyone to participate in them. In the presence of this music, passionate on the one hand, simple and precise on the other, conveying an experience both personal and shared by society, the problem of the individual versus society – source of all our present-day intellectual crises – loses all meaning.

Beethoven's music thus stands as a triumphant testimony to the power of unity and concord, the fusion of the language of music with the language of the soul, of formal structure with the portrayal of human drama, above all of the individual with the universe, the frightened soul with the community of mankind. 'Brothers, there must be a loving Father dwelling above the starry firmament!' cried Schiller. When Beethoven used these words in the Finale of his Ninth Symphony, he was not playing the role of a preacher, still less of a demagogue. He was simply being what he had always been, right from the beginning. That is why he still has the power to move us today.

7 Mendelssohn

Enough has been said and written about Mendelssohn's association with Leipzig, and although, as a former conductor of the Gewandhaus orchestra, I am one of his successors, I shall not concern myself with that subject here. Nor was it the reason, or the only reason, why I particularly welcomed the invitation to share in these centennial celebrations. There are more profound causes to recall today what Mendelssohn was and what he achieved.

It is not all that long ago that a bigoted racist doctrine denied that Mendelssohn was a German composer. Yet to any objective observer there cannot be the slightest doubt about the matter. To be sure, unlike Mahler, who belongs to no less a degree to the German cultural scene, Mendelssohn does not belong in a narrow German frame of reference, for during his lifetime his presence was felt all over Europe. But the influences upon him, like the influence he himself exerted, and the models he adopted, were all essentially German. His place is without question in the history of German music. He is one of the most fertile, most striking examples of the symbiosis of German-ness and Jewish-ness, and gives the lie to those theories which hold that such a symbiosis is impossible or, if not impossible, then undesirable. A central work in the programme that I am due to conduct in the Gewandhaus on the centennial of his death is the Eroica Symphony, that greatest piece of universal, yet at the same time German, hero-worship. And fittingly so, for in his own way Mendelssohn is an heroic figure in the history of German music, and we do not need the chance occasion of an anniversary in order to remind ourselves of the fact.

The famous violinist Carl Flesch, himself a Jew, once said to me: 'Mendelssohn is the leading composer in the second rank'. In other words, although he has a prominent position, he cannot be ranked among the very greatest. It is a judgement confirmed by history. Many of his works have faded from view, lost in the mists of the past, leaving only a few survivors – though these few display an amazing mastery and originality.

However, I do not wish to talk about Mendelssohn in the narrower context, as a composer who will always be regarded as having his own particular, if limited significance at a certain moment in the course of German Romantic music. Of works with the originality and spontaneity of the music to *A Midsummer Night's Dream* he wrote but few. But that is not the end of the matter. More important, to my mind, and in a sense more relevant to the present age, is his role as the founder of a school, the creator of a cultural synthesis. Schumann, the finest of the German Romantics, discoverer of new values, a man who saw far beyond the confines of his immediate environment, looked up to him with boundless admiration as the representative of a living tradition.

This is a point at which we should pause. Tradition is a concept whose meaning we have to a large extent forgotten. Since the onset of the modern revolution in music, the permanent revolution, the beginnings of which can be traced back to the 'music of the future' of Wagner and Liszt, the emotional appeal of tradition has grown weaker and weaker. People have forgotten that tradition can be the most powerful of forces. The emotional appeal of revolution has taken over, so much so that people no longer know what to revolt against.[1]

The tradition that Mendelssohn represents is in a very special sense the tradition of German music. It was he who created that synthesis which arose from the foundations laid by Bach, Beethoven and the other German Classical composers. The Leipzig conservatoire,[2] which he founded, dominated the nineteenth century, and its roots lay in that immortal German music that has conquered the world. In the second half of the century the supremacy of the Mendelssohn school was continued by Joachim,[3] praised by no less a man than Wagner as an outstanding musician both as performer and teacher, and behind whom stood the figure of Brahms. It is also to Mendelssohn that we owe the rediscovery of Bach and the first performance of the St Matthew Passion since Bach's own day.[4] Bach on the one side, Beethoven's symphonies on the other – such were his parameters, art at its greatest, relevant to the age, subject to timeless laws.

What Mendelssohn found embodied in this music was the principle of artistic laws, in the highest sense. The Leipzig conservatoire taught laws – narrow laws, perhaps, but real laws nonetheless. True, we must be under no illusion that such laws can be easily abused; pedants of all kinds have both done so and continue to do so. But today we have a different attitude towards these laws. Symbols of tradition, they represent a rejection, a fundamental rejection, of individualism. The laws that Mendelssohn followed were the laws of convention, and if one is to criticize his music, the first thing to say is that it is conventional.

But it is not only conventional. Or, more accurately, it is not really an expression of convention at all. For central to the laws that Mendelssohn follows is something that we have totally lost sight of today – I would call it 'the category of naturalness'.[5] It is this quality – found also in Brahms, Smetana, Tchaikovsky, Schumann, and many others, including even Wagner – that predominates in his music.

Mendelssohn, Joachim, Schenker, Mahler – they are both Jews and Germans. They testify that we Germans have every reason to see ourselves as a great and noble people. How tragic that this has to be emphasized today.[6]

8 Wagner

a) On the Music of Wagner's *Ring des Nibelungen*

The *Ring des Nibelungen* has always been Wagner's most controversial work. On the one hand it never achieved the popularity
of his early works, on the other it was never able to win the
approval of musicians to the extent of *Tristan und Isolde* or *Die
Meistersinger von Nürnberg*. All opposition to Wagner was from
the outset directed primarily at the *Ring*.

The differences between the *Ring* and Wagner's other works
are not all that easy to identify. If we take *Tristan* or *Die Meistersinger*, we are aware from the very beginning of something
which gives the whole work, heterogeneous though it is, a quite
extraordinary unity. There is an all-enveloping atmosphere that
permeates every pore of the work, a mysterious nucleus from
which energy spreads to every corner. This is the source of the
characteristic musical style peculiar to each individual work.
Starting in the Prelude, a microcosm of the meaning of the work
as a whole, it retains its power to the very last bars.

But the *Ring* has no such central nucleus. Not that it does
not have its own style – but it is a different style from that
found in Wagner's other works. There we find ourselves from
the beginning in a poetic atmosphere, an atmosphere breathed
by human beings, which sets the tone and spirit of the action.
In the *Ring*, on the other hand, the plot develops laboriously
from a multitude of individual elements – the gods, the giants,
the dwarfs, the depths of the Rhine, the caves of Nibelheim –
which at first sight seem to be there more for their own sake
than that of the flimsy action that barely manages to hold them
together. Only gradually does the human dimension come to
occupy the scene, first with Siegmund and Sieglinde, and ultimately with the idealized figure of Siegfried.

Yet even this takes place against the background of a world
of mythical creatures and supernatural forces which is no substi-

tute for the poetic reality that informs the yearning for love and death in *Tristan* and the serene radiance of *Die Meistersinger*. At least, it is no substitute as far as Wagner the composer is concerned. For he needs this poetic reality, this basis of human experience, this centrally-inspired atmosphere and mood, in order to create his music. Here lies the real source of his strength. It is this that he floods with his music, creating with all the means at his disposal an experience of living reality. What may be called the central idea of the *Ring*, on the other hand – the theft of the gold and the sequence of disasters that follows – remains an idea, an intellectual construct, abstract, and thus beyond the reach of music.

This brings about a radical change in the function of the music. It now becomes much more closely linked with the dramatic action than in Wagner's other works. The music does not proceed in the background, parallel to the events and characters on the stage but actually *becomes* those events and characters itself – the gods, heroes, dwarfs, the fire, the water and the rest. It is tied to the individual moment and everything is subordinated to the interests of explicitness. It is the most absolute theatre music imaginable, and gives birth to that series of concentrated Leitmotifs, basic to the point of abstraction, which have so impressed themselves on the public's mind.

Strictly speaking, in the context of the drama as a whole these motifs derive their meaning only from their first appearance, accompanying the events on the stage. They stand isolated, they do not lead anywhere, do not generate a creative atmosphere around themselves, like the main themes of so many works. They are in the nature of mnemonics, or units of construction.

Nowhere is this technique of the Leitmotif more consistently employed than in the later sections of the *Ring* cycle. The music acquires an out-and-out decorative character, seen especially in the orchestration – hence the size of the orchestral forces employed. Unlike in other operas, where his principal concern is with the production of an all-enveloping, homogeneous musical sound, Wagner here aims at the creation of a wealth of individual effects, exploiting the colours of the tonal palette in all their characteristic brilliance. The music has abandoned all attempt to retain its absolute, self-sufficient character and avoids as far as it can all forms of a purely musical nature. Its design is loose, often non-committal, sometimes consisting of little more than fragments stuck together in a rough-and-ready way.

Instead of grand symphonic structures we find large-scale sound-paintings, like Siegfried's Journey down the Rhine or the funeral march from *Götterdämmerung*.

There is today a widespread opposition to Wagner which is far more than just a reaction against the exaggerated Wagner-worship of an earlier age. The 'true' musician and the 'true' poet resent the devaluation of their art that accompanies the concept of the *Gesamtkunstwerk*. Not only this, but in the last analysis Wagner is denied the right to call himself an artist at all, since his work is not organic and unified, not pure and simple like that of all the world's great artists but cobbled together from the most heterogeneous sources, decked out with all manner of ostentatious effects, some of them artistic, others not, and playing on the most disparate instincts of his public. And of all his works the *Ring* is the one that attracts the greatest criticism on these scores, criticism evoked by the change in the function of the music, its closer involvement with the action on the stage and its corresponding loss of independent meaning.

But this is to overlook that Wagner is here pursuing a different goal than in his other works. Taken as a whole the *Ring* is a surface, so to speak, rather than a centre, diffuse rather than concentrated. But what a sensuous, glowing surface! What power, what vivid intensity in those visions of Valhalla, the Ride of the Valkyries, the conflagration! What the music loses in unity and logical purpose it gains in immediacy of effect. Would the monumental grandeur of the tetralogy, the headlong pace of *Die Walküre*, the unbridled freedom of *Siegfried*, the colossal proportions of *Götterdämmerung* be possible but for the dazzling music that sustains the mythological world where these superhuman figures dwell?

Finally and most vitally – the dramas of the *Ring* must be seen as their author puts them before us. This is not the place to enter into a discussion of the complex and never properly expounded concept of the *Gesamtkunstwerk*, a concept which Wagner himself did more to obfuscate than anyone else. This much, however, must be said – that it is one single mind behind this multiplicity of forms and forces, one single will directing all their manifestations. It is a simple, direct will, of a piece, like that behind all great art. All the different means employed – music, text, singer, producer – only receive their meaning in the context of the total work of art, the essence of which is, in the broadest sense, poetic. The voice of the creator of the work is a poetic voice that rings out loud and clear. But it will not do so if the work is turned into a symphony, or a psychological drama, or – perish the thought – a stage spectacular.

This is why it is of such overwhelming importance that the *Ring* be properly performed. The moment individual elements are allowed to thrust themselves into the limelight – the producer at the expense of the orchestra, or the orchestra at the expense of the singers – the occasion will deteriorate into a jumble of bits and pieces, a thoroughly inartistic *mélange* which will be grist to the mill of Wagner's opponents. To a greater degree than any other of his works, a misconceived performance of the *Ring* can lead to a totally false impression of the work.

Guidelines for a proper interpretation can only come from the music, for it is the music that is Wagner's sharpest tool, the most direct, most subtle medium for the expression of his supreme thoughts, that which embodies the essence of the work. Every movement, every scene both emerges from, and returns to, the music. It is thus the musician who is charged with the real responsibility for seeing that Wagner's artistic will be done.

b)   The Case of Wagner

Wagner is the most highly controversial figure in the entire history of the arts. The impact made by his work on his contemporaries is hard to describe – and the concept of 'success', in the conventional sense, is quite inapplicable. Scarcely ever has an artist caused such agitation among his fellow-men, or his works had such a revolutionary effect. And scarcely ever has an artist been met with so much suspicion, so much sullen antipathy. Great as was the affection and veneration that he commanded, equally great was the bitter, sometimes petulant hostility that he was made to endure.

To be sure, we find similar situations with other great figures. The arrival of something new always provokes conflicts of opinion. But not only is the controversy that rages round Wagner particularly violent, it has also lasted far longer than other such controversies. One might go so far as to say that it is no less heated today than it was in Wagner's own age. People continue to be divided, particularly in Germany, into those who are for him and those who are against him. He seems to be an exception to the general belief that later generations pass more far-sighted, more accurate and fairer judgements on an artist than do his contemporaries. The 'Case of Wagner' is as live an issue today as it was in Nietzsche's time, and we have hardly moved one step forward in the sixty years since Wagner's death. Is it so difficult to establish the necessary critical distance between him and us?

Whatever the opinions about Wagner may be, the power of his works, and in particular of his music, still remains extraordinary. He dominates the opera houses of the world, from Paris to Rome, from London to New York. Apart from those of Verdi and Puccini his operas are the only operas still alive in our theatres, in spite of the extraordinary demands they make on the listener and the no less extraordinary difficulties they pose for the performers. His music is more popular than serious music of this kind has ever been, and addresses itself to people of all classes and all levels of education. It is played in concerts for highbrow intellectuals no less than in open-air concerts and military bandstands.

Yet in spite of all this, the opposition to him has persisted. As far as his contemporaries are concerned, this is understandable. The novelty of his works – or, more accurately, of the approach that they demanded of his listeners – made it difficult to comprehend them. Their peculiar amalgamation of poetry, music and dramatic action had no precedent. Wagner had no predecessors – any more, strictly speaking, than he has had any successors. Anybody who brought aesthetic concepts to bear on the *Gesamtkunstwerk* derived from the individual arts seen in isolation was bound to end up in a state of confusion. The only ones to find access to him were those who surrendered themselves to him without further ado. And they, moreover, discovered that, far from being an agglomeration of elements, his works, like all true art, are homogeneous entities, albeit built up of a great variety of different elements. Yet we still find men of letters sneering at Wagner the poet and conceding, at the most, the legitimacy of Wagner the composer. At the same time musicians, particularly those with their roots in so-called absolute music, turn their backs on him and call him an anti-composer, a defiler of pure music.

These were not the only reasons for the opposition to Wagner. The disapproval, the contempt, and ultimately the hatred affected by his contemporaries was aimed rather at the man than at his works, especially in Germany. We still feel the after-effects of this today. Envy has always been one of the Germans' strong suits. Over the years they have waged persistent smear campaigns against Wagner, refusing to accept that the man in whose drawer the score of *Tristan und Isolde* lay could not be expected to behave like any Tom, Dick or Harry. They were not prepared to concede that this man, who, to speak in purely economic terms, had inspired a turnover of millions – an achievement hardly matched by any other artist – had the right to approach his friends for money and canvass support for his work. No artist was ever so savagely attacked and vilified; every little thing about him was made an object of derision, down to the silk dressing-gowns which, because of their associations, he chose to wear while working. When King Ludwig of Bavaria espoused his cause, the whole country united in taking up arms against him. And despite all efforts, including those of his royal patron, it never became possible to found a conservatoire under his directorship – an undertaking which would have made no great demands on state funds and would have brought incalculable benefits to the musical life of Germany.

Yet despite this his works gradually began to establish themselves. People found themselves unable to resist the power of their impact. Still the opposition did not slacken – indeed, its pace even seemed to quicken and its success to multiply.

At this moment there emerged a figure whose fate was to become remarkably and inextricably entwined with Wagner's, a figure who was to make himself the spokesman of all those who harboured anti-Wagnerian resentment of any kind, and whose name has remained inseparable from Wagner ever since. I speak of Friedrich Nietzsche.

In his early career Nietzsche was completely under Wagner's spell. His first work, *The Birth of Tragedy from the Spirit of Music*, takes Wagner as its starting-point and ends as a hymn of praise to his hero.[1] The essays called *Thoughts Out Of Season* that followed also stand in the shadow of Wagner, the last of them, *Richard Wagner in Bayreuth*, summarizing his thoughts down to that moment.

Wagner had recognized Nietzsche's talent from the beginning and sought to engage it in the promotion of his own cause with the ruthless egoism characteristic of him. Liszt, Bülow, Cornelius, Nietzsche – they were all there to further his own purposes, serve the interests of his own works. He could never view them in any other light. One has to remember this if one is to understand the history of the relationship between him and Nietzsche.

As the world sees the situation, Wagner is by far the less likeable of the two, neither accepting the genuine offer of friendship that the younger man made him nor even making an effort to appreciate its true value. But the practical world is a hard world. And if he were to fulfil his mission, Wagner too had to be hard. However unpleasant it may have been for those immediately affected by it, we must concede that his egoism was thoroughly justified, even necessary. He was compelled to act thus – his works are his vindication.

This is not to deny that Nietzsche too was driven by his own inner compulsion and followed the laws of his own development. But if we put ourselves in Wagner's place, can we say that Nietzsche, especially the young Nietzsche, had such a power of personality as to be able to command from Wagner the feeling that he was dealing with an equal? We know from other instances that Wagner was fully capable of such feelings. He could not have been the composer he was if he had not acknowledged the truth of such situations. We know how he felt about Beethoven, and later about Schopenhauer. That he did not feel the same way about Nietzsche is no cause for surprise. Nietzsche's mind was too dependent, too full of thoughts inspired by Wagner himself for the older man to accept the originality of his views, even on remote subjects like the Greeks. He could not see him other than as a pupil, a disciple, the more so as Nietzsche was a sensitive, highly-strung young man who in his personal dealings often displayed more sympathy for other people's views than actually corresponded to his inner convictions. He never had the assertiveness to push his opinions in conversation with a man like Wagner. When subsequently putting his thoughts on paper, however, this assertiveness manifested itself with redoubled strength. But for all this he remained the younger and more dependent partner, and experienced far more suffering in the course of the whole relationship than did Wagner. The world tends to sympathize with the weaker party in such cases. Here it is not a matter of sympathy but of the facts of the situation and of justification. And if we are honest, we cannot deny that Wagner had this justification.

As we mentioned above, Nietzsche's early works are all dominated in one way or another by Wagner. In *The Birth of Tragedy* he claimed to find in Greek tragedy the predecessor of Wagner's *Gesamtkunstwerk*, and in the figure of Socrates the spiritual confusion and the decline of instinctual certainty characteristic of his own age. Wagner, his works and his adversaries are all translated to the world of Classical Antiquity as part of Nietzsche's conception that Antiquity, indeed the whole of history, derives its basic meaning from its relationship to the present. He sees the opposition to Socrates as the equivalent, in different circumstances and in a different form, of the struggle waged by Wagner against the intellectual Philistines in Germany. This struggle, which can be traced in a variety of forms through all the *Thoughts Out Of Season*, is one of the dominant concerns of the young Nietzsche.

Wagner was the centre of Nietzsche's intellectual universe, the point from which he took his bearings. It was not so much a matter of understanding Wagner himself and his works, using them to help him understand the world, his own world, which was by definition broader in scope than Wagner's. Rather, he saw Wagner as the background against which everything had to be viewed, the perspective he required in order to acquire his own knowledge. Wagner, for his part, saw Nietzsche in the first place as a writer on himself – possibly the best and greatest such writer – and considered himself fully entitled to expect him to continue serving the cause of his music. But as time went on, with Wagner making these demands and with Nietzsche continually trying to escape from them, while making Wagner into the kind of figure that he needed for his own development, the relationship between the two men became increasingly strained. Nietzsche kept his distance out of a sense of self-preservation, of loyalty to himself. Wagner was the considerably more active, the more forthcoming as far as personal contact was concerned. It was inevitable that tensions would develop between them in the course of time. Wagner could not but realize that here was someone who was not following closely enough the path that had been laid down for him, not doing quite what was expected of him.

Richard Wagner in Bayreuth, the last of the *Thoughts Out Of Season*, may be regarded as the product of a kind of implicit duress exercised by Wagner over Nietzsche.[2] Nietzsche needed to do something in order to avoid betraying the expectations of Bayreuth, and therefore decided to make this essay a summary of his boundless admiration for the man who had illuminated the course of his life and thought down to that moment. Hitherto Wagner had represented for him an ideal, a vision whose radiance had shone from afar; now he found himself forced to give an account of this vision, to analyse it – precisely what he had instinctively avoided doing. The particular interest in this essay for us lies in the fact that, written at a time when Nietzsche was still free of suspicion, still governed by affection, it gives us a number of insights into the nature of his relationship with Wagner about which his later works, full of accusations and recriminations, are silent. At the same time he seems inhibited by the thought that Wagner himself would be one of his readers. His language is forced, his style, despite his evident gifts, curiously contorted. The influence of Wagner seems to be everywhere – the emotionalism is Wagner's, the accent is Wagner's. At hardly any other time do we find Nietzsche so cramped, so constrained as at this moment, when he sets out to erect a monument to the man he had so profoundly loved and revered. In fact he talks more about himself than about his hero, more about the hopes and apprehensions that Wagner's works arouse in him than about those works themselves. Everything is made to relate to Wagner.

And it is above all Wagner the man whose presence one feels. For great as was Wagner the creative artist for the young Nietzsche, still greater was the man behind the works, the man whose life was shot through with a terrible sense of dissatisfaction that could not be soothed either by the joys of success or by a retreat into isolation. History, philosophy, human knowledge – nothing could withstand the titanic power of his will. Driven forward by his inner daemon, he sought nothing less than the spiritual renewal of mankind, to teach men how to regain the use of their feelings, to restore their lost innocence.

What Wagner experienced in life is given artistic shape in his works. In *The Birth of Tragedy* Nietzsche is principally concerned to provide a justification for a tragic conception of life, and Bayreuth represented for him the artistic embodiment of tragedy, the renewal of the tragic theatre of Antiquity, with Wagner as the 'Dionysian dramatist'. In his own words:

> The greatness and the indispensability of art reside in the fact that it gives us a premonition of a simpler world, of a simpler solution to the enigma of life. No one who undergoes the pain of life can survive without this premonition, any more than anyone can survive without sleep. The harder it becomes to understand life, the more fervently we yearn to glimpse this premonition, if only for a moment, and the greater the tension becomes between our overall perception of things and our intellectual and moral capacity as individuals. Art is there to prevent the bow from snapping.

Art as consolation for the man suffering the pain of life, as a means of survival, as indispensable as sleep. Is not Nietzsche here glorifying those very qualities that he later found so despicable, so abhorrent in Wagner?

In all this Nietzsche felt that he was not being entirely true to himself. He was not suited to the role of mere panegyrist, as others were, and as Wagner expected him to be. He felt uneasy and began to have doubts about publishing *Richard Wagner in Bayreuth* even while he was still working on it. He wrote to his friend Erwin Rohde:

> My reflections entitled *Richard Wagner in Bayreuth* will not be published. They are almost finished but I have utterly failed to live up to my own expectations, so that their only value for me is that of a kind of guide to help me over the most critical stage of our relationship. I am unsure of myself and realize that I have not yet managed to find a true sense of direction – quite apart from being in a position to help others to find it.

Subsequently, having added a few new chapters, Nietzsche allowed himself to be persuaded by others and with an eye to the approaching festival in Bayreuth in 1876 – to submit the work for publication.

But these later chapters are different in tone and character from their predecessors. Here for the first time Nietzsche attempts to talk about Wagner himself, to give a reasoned account of his achievements. Under three headings – Wagner as Poet, Wagner as Composer and Wagner as Writer – he sets out what Wagner meant to him. So characteristic are his remarks on Wagner's poetic language that I cannot resist quoting from them here. 'There runs through Wagner's poetry,' he writes,

> a delight in language, an openness and warmth, such as is to be experienced in no other German poet except Goethe – concrete imagery, bold elliptical constructions, power of expression and variety of rhythm, an astonishing wealth of forceful vocabulary, the use of a simplified syntax, an inventiveness, almost unmatched, in the language of passion and premonition, and at the same time a vein of popular joviality and earthiness.

Nietzsche was, of course, fully aware that none of Wagner's dramas was intended to be read or could be made subject to criteria applicable to drama. When reading Wagner's libretti one must always remember that the reification of the dramatic action is conveyed through three media – poetry, gesture and music. If we are to do justice to Wagner the dramatist, we must keep this totality in mind.

What Nietzsche has to say about Wagner the composer is less interesting, less original. He follows the same avenues of thought as Wagner himself had already laid out. When Wagner wrote about his music, his obvious intention was to explain and justify its function. In pointing out how different it was from the music of earlier periods, he was only stating a fact. And in seeing himself as a goal, the final link in an historical chain of development, he was being entirely accurate. At the same time he made it clear time and again – in his essay on Beethoven, for instance – that he was fully conversant with the essence of the music of his predecessors. It never occurred to him to compare his music with theirs.

But his followers reacted differently – including Nietzsche, who, swept off his feet by Wagner's music, joined the ranks of those who regarded music pre-Wagner as merely preparing the way of the Master, as offering but a faint inkling of what was to come. On Wagner's music itself Nietzsche has a number of apposite observations to make, such as that here we find aspects of nature – sunrise, forests, mists, mountain-tops, the terrors of the night and so on – portrayed in music for the first time. But when he talks of earlier composers, it is in tones that show how completely his ear is attuned to Wagner's, how utterly Wagner has 'perverted' him. Nietzsche appears not to recognize that music can create an organic, self-contained world from its own inner resources, a world with as absolute a validity as that created by Wagner in his *Gesamtkunstwerk*, of which music is only a part.

On Wagner the essay-writer and critic Nietzsche comments:

> I know of no writing on the arts that sheds so much light on the subject as Wagner's. Whatever can be learned about the genesis of a work of art is to be found here. It is one of the very greatest of minds that we encounter in these pages, and over the years he has been constantly refining his theories, stating his views with ever greater freedom and clarity.

And on the subject of the significance of Wagner's art *in toto* he concludes:

> This is not art aimed at the cultivation of an élite. It knows nothing of a distinction between the educated and the uneducated. As such it stands in stark contrast to the culture of the Renaissance, in the shadow of which we had hitherto been nurtured.

Wagner stands, in other words, as a victor, the supreme conqueror of the Renaissance and everything to which it has given rise. In so saying, Nietzsche reveals as much of his true relationship to Wagner as do his later diatribes. He shows himself to be what I would call a typical Wagnerite – a term whose meaning will emerge later.

Richard Wagner in Bayreuth was completed in June 1876. In August Nietzsche attended the festival and experienced his first great disappointment – beginning with the audiences. What a contrast to that chosen few of whom Wagner had once dreamed and Nietzsche had written in his essay! Nothing but a typical first-night audience! And worst of all, Wagner himself seemed quite impervious to it all. Was it perhaps an utopian image of Wagner that he had created? Was this the sober reality that now confronted him?

Wagner saw all too clearly what caused Nietzsche such mortification. But he was an artist, that is, a man of action, not an idealist, and was accustomed to adapt himself to circumstances. When Nietzsche sent him a copy of his essay, he cabled back: 'It is a tremendous piece of work.' Wagner was satisfied. But what about Nietzsche? It was only two months since he had completed his essay but now, at the first festival in Bayreuth, it felt to him like five years, and he was reluctant to talk about it.

A parting of the ways became more and more inevitable. Events took their course, events that need not detain us here, save to note that we only have Nietzsche's reactions to them. What Wagner thought about the man who had suddenly turned his back on him, we do not know. Nietzsche wrote *The Case of Wagner* but Wagner wrote no *Case of Nietzsche*.

Initially Nietzsche held his peace. Only many years later, after Wagner's death, did he publish the works that revealed the one-time admirer and worshipper as an antagonist more frightening and more destructive than almost any other artist has been made to endure.

At the time *Richard Wagner in Bayreuth* suffered the same fate as virtually all writings on Wagner, namely, they were read only by Wagnerites or those who took an interest in the composer. By the time of *The Case of Wagner* Nietzsche's own career was in the ascendant. Here, moreover, he addressed himself to the public at large, and in particular to those who had no connection with Wagner. Another significant consideration was that he had formerly been one of Wagner's most passionate and eloquent disciples, a man of whom it could hardly be said that he did not know the man he was attacking.

One of the first things to strike us about *The Case of Wagner* is its aggressive tone, often degenerating into mockery, even open hatred. Thinking back for a moment to their earlier friendship, we may wonder whether such a tone was necessary. We know that Nietzsche was very sensitive about personal matters. There are remarkable examples of his inability to distinguish between his personal likes and dislikes and objective judgements. One such case was that of his disciple and flatterer Peter Gast – a man nowhere near his intellectual equal – whose trivial compositions he held up as being the only really great music of the time. Another example is his behaviour towards Brahms, whom he praised for a while at the expense of Wagner but later, after Brahms had returned without comment a composition that he, Nietzsche, had sent him, lost no opportunity to belittle. It was the price that Brahms, with his incorruptible honesty, was made to pay for delivering his frank and singleminded judgement.

So we are left with the question: What could have happened to cause Nietzsche to feel that his only recourse was to write works like *The Case of Wagner*? Could it have been because of Wagner's growing success, because it was evident that his works had won the day? It was part of Nietzsche's nature that he could only function effectively when opposing something. He held up a mirror to his age and criticized what he saw. As long as Wagner was not yet famous and had to overcome narrow-mindedness and antipathy, Nietzsche stood shoulder to shoulder with him in the struggle against the self-styled *cognoscenti*. But now the struggle was over. These *cognoscenti* had been forced to come over to Wagner's side, and Nietzsche had to find another level on which to renew his assault, even at the price of antagonizing the man he had once revered.

The Case of Wagner had the effect that Nietzsche sought. Its impact was immense. It was as though all those who had been nursing some grudge against Wagner had just been waiting for a spokesman to put their feelings into words, and the appearance of this work marks the real beginning of the hostility towards Wagner. It set the tone for all anti-Wagnerian criticism, and practically everything that has been written against Wagner in the last sixty years is little more than a feeble reiteration of what Nietzsche said.

At any particular time Nietzsche's thinking would be dominated by certain key ideas. In *The Birth of Tragedy*, as we have seen, he was preoccupied with his crusade against rationalism, pursued against the background of Greek tragedy and its modern reincarnation in the work of Wagner. Although this idea never completely disappeared, it gave way to others as Wagner's dominance waned, in particular to the dynamic concept of the rise and fall of moral and cultural values according to innate laws. It was a concept based on an analogy with biological principles, and its special fascination for Nietzsche – always the man with his gaze focused on his own age – lay in its relevance to a problem characteristic of that age, *viz.* the problem of degeneration and decadence. He became obsessed with the prospect of being able to use this newly-discovered concept in order to identify and explain a whole mass of phenomena whose significance had hitherto eluded him. As Spengler later said of himself, it was not that he possessed an idea but that the idea possessed him. Nietzsche the moralist now felt able at last to tear the veil from the things that had worried and depressed him and reveal their true nature. The road that led to the destruction of false values – the 'twilight of the idols', as he called it, in an ironical pun on Wagner's *Twilight of the Gods*[3] – now lay open before him, a road that was to lead him to the gates of Christianity.

Today the situation does not appear to us to be so straightforward. The individual represents a sample, a cross-section of the multitude of strands that run through life, intersecting to form innumerable different patterns. To be sure, when viewed from a distance, individual epochs appear to follow their own path of development, their own destiny. But here too it is not so easy to give a simple interpretation of the situation in the way Spengler did, for example. There are numerous different impulses at work, and currents can flow in different directions. To take one example out of many: although Bach lived and worked in the Baroque age, his music has nothing to do with Baroque. The spirit of his music is the purest Gothic.

We have become particularly cautious, moreover, about making over-hasty judgements concerning the age whose values are the most difficult to interpret, the most complex, most heterogeneous of all ages – the present. No longer can we, like Nietzsche, lump all its various manifestations together under the catchword 'decadence'. Indeed, Nietzsche himself found himself forced by his own slogan to declare as decadent not only Wagner, and not only himself, with all his ideas, powers and desires but also the politically conscious men and women of his time and the achievements of the nations around him. He thus attached no importance to the Franco-Prussian War or the foundation of the Second Reich in 1871.

It was predictable that Nietzsche would use his concept of decadence as the key to his interpretation of Wagner. What he had formerly praised as positive qualities he now portrayed as negative, albeit not without occasionally doing considerable violence to the facts. 'Wagner's is a sick art,' he wrote. 'The problems he portrays on the stage are the problems of hysterical creatures, and his heroes and heroines, seen in human terms, are a morbid procession of invalids.' And he goes on:

> This is the very source of Wagner's success. His works are a seductive mixture of what today's world seeks, the three great stimuli of the tired and jaded, *viz.* brutality, artificiality and childish folly.

Nietzsche totally overlooks that Wagner is an artist who has the whole of life spread out in front of him, life as it is, with characters who reflect the many different aspects of reality. For a man obsessed with the concept of decadence to describe it in terms of sickness and health is far from doing justice to the subject. In fact, many of Wagner's characters are, in this sense, extremely healthy – Siegfried, for example, whom Nietzsche himself called an exception among Wagner's heroes, or the Mastersingers, every one of whom literally radiates health and vigour. And even those who are possessed, or who live under the shadow of a brooding fate, or who, like Tristan and Isolde, become transported into another world – they all share in that higher 'healthiness' innate in all Wagner's characters, the strength to live true, fulfilled lives, to bear their yoke and to be totally themselves in all that they do.

Twelve years after *Richard Wagner in Bayreuth* we find Nietzsche proceeding in *The Case of Wagner* rather in the manner of a lawyer who collects all the information he needs for his case, interprets it to suit his own purposes, and ignores everything else. Eloquent as he can be, now as then, he also knows how to keep silent when it is in his interest to do so. Or were all the things he had said about Wagner in the past simply wrong, pure fantasy? At all events he now diligently selects from the evidence the points that strike him as open to attack, points which his love-hate relationship to his subject enables him to identify with uncanny ease. The target of his thrusts is now Wagner's music. What he admires in this music, he says, is the composer's skill in dealing with the particular, his attention to detail; in this regard Wagner is 'a master of the highest rank, the greatest miniaturist in music, who can compress an infinity of meaning and charm into the smallest of spaces'. Everything else he calls into question. The essence of this music lies in what he terms the external 'gesture'. This is the alpha and omega of the whole enterprise. How awkward, how pitiful, he exclaims, are Wagner's attempts at musical development! The man has nothing in common with real composers, let alone with great composers, because he is incapable of creating an artistic whole; his music is wild, undisciplined, bereft of inner structure.

How shrewd of Nietzsche suddenly to conjure up the image of the 'real', 'great' composers and to talk about structure, discipline and organic 'artistic wholes'! When he needs the great composers as a measure of judgement or as a contrast to Wagner, he is prepared to invoke their name but his own relationship to them was a singularly loose one. He was, of course, what one calls 'musical'. He composed music himself.[4] But the really great names left little mark on him, and in his prolix way he makes this amply clear. His remarks on Bach and Beethoven are cool, detached and reveal a total absence of any profound understanding of their works. Beethoven he regards simply as a representative of the eighteenth century, his most attractive quality being his ability to 'express in music his happiness, in the autumn of his life, over a love now past'. (One wonders which works Nietzsche had in mind when he produced this strange definition.)

In truth Nietzsche was not concerned with the organic principle in music or with questions of structure. What attracted him in music were its colours, its fragrance, its delicacy, its sensuous, morbid, transient, seductive qualities. He once declared that he would 'give the whole of the rest of music' for Chopin – not, of course, for that which sets Chopin among the great figures in music but for Chopin, the unique creator of delicate perfumes. Right to the end of his days Nietzsche remained the Wagnerian that he had been from the beginning. Nor could it be otherwise. Whatever else may evolve in the course of one's life, one can do nothing to change one's fundamental relationship to art, embedded, as it is, in the depths of our subconscious.

The most problematical aspect of Wagner's work is the theory of the *Gesamtkunstwerk*, i.e. how the constituent elements in this composite work of art come together to form a unity. A large proportion of Wagner's own writings is devoted to analysing and answering this question, since it was here, he felt, that most of the misconceptions would arise.

So this was where Nietzsche decided to launch his main assault. Wagner's *Gesamtkunstwerk*, he maintained, was an omnium gatherum, a conglomeration of elements amassed by the sweat of his brow, not a work that had grown organically from natural beginnings or been rigorously planned and executed by a central intelligence. So what held this massive structure together – for there must be some determined controlling force behind it?

In his answer to this question Nietzsche delivered what he hoped would be his most crushing blow. This whole artificial concoction called *Gesamtkunstwerk*, he proclaimed, owed its existence to Wagner's penchant for theatricality, for ostentation. No longer was Wagner the 'Dionysian dramatist', as he had once called him; no longer was he a poet; no longer was he even a composer. He was a play-actor, a Thespian, the greatest illusionist the world had ever seen. The whole enterprise had its base in the theatre, it was on the theatre that it depended, and it was the theatre that proved his undoing. Whether he was playing the role of poet, or composer, or philosopher, or assuming any other function, in the last analysis he did not move outside the theatre, the home of play-acting.

But play-acting, Nietzsche went on, is a form of lying, and the situation is at its worst when an actor begins to believe his own lies. *The Case of Wagner* ends with the following words: 'My love of art forces me to make three demands: that the theatre shall not be allowed to dominate the other arts; that actors shall not be allowed to deceive those of honest mind; and that music shall not be allowed to become an art that lies'.

Devil's advocate, driven by hate, Nietzsche struck home with this accusation. By exposing Wagner as an actor – which to the Germans, for whom the theatre frequently has something of a dubious reputation, was tantamount to calling him a confidence trickster – he deprived him at a stroke of that which every artist most desperately needs if his work is to be well received – trust and confidence. In the eyes of the world Wagner stood condemned – not a poet, not a composer, in fact not an artist of any importance at all. And as an actor, a man of the theatre – here the argument returns to its starting-point – Wagner is the paradigmatic decadent, the most perfect and most instructive embodiment of artistic degeneration that one could ask for. It is precisely because, in his own way, he had a naive faith in his play-acting as though it were the truth, that one can so readily identify in his works all the characteristic features of decadence. If it were necessary to select one of these features as the most evident and most decisive, it would have to be the piecemeal, conglomerative nature of his works. Behind the play-acting is a desire for effect – effect for its own sake and at any price, one effect after another, leading to an accumulation of effects the like of which had not remotely been seen before. That is why Wagner was so successful. But this success is in its turn just one more token of the decadence of his art.

Nietzsche knew full well – perhaps all too well – what artistic decadence was. The enthusiasm and ingenuity that he develops in the course of his quest give him away. Indeed, he once came out with the admission, in his forthright, uncompromising way, that he was a decadent himself, like Wagner; as a spokesman for his age, he could hardly be other. Everything that he blames Wagner for being, he is himself. *He* is the writer who works piecemeal, the aphorist who cannot create coherent large-scale works, and does not wish to. *He* is the lover of nuances, of delicate and fleeting moments, of rare, often impenetrable emotions. And he certainly did not concede anything to Wagner as far as a desire for effect was concerned. This is shown no less by his style than by his success – a success which, if one uses his own argument, testifies as much against him as it does against Wagner.

Both men are typical examples of decadence. But there is a difference between them. Wagner has a naive belief in himself and is unaware of his decadence; Nietzsche, on the other hand, more truthful and more honest – in his own eyes – *is* aware of it. But his awareness does not alter the fact. The knowledge that I am sick does not make me healthy. It does, however, have one consequence – it causes me to take a different view of myself. This is why the decadent artist is so often unable to tolerate himself. That so many people today are attracted to the music of epochs long past – those of Bach and Mozart, for instance – can often be traced to this condition. They take refuge in the past because they cannot bear the present, and they do their utmost to put themselves, and everything connected with themselves, out of their minds in order to avoid confronting their own reality. When Nietzsche vents his ire on Wagner, he is venting it on himself. Wagner is his undoing but he cannot escape from him, because he cannot escape from himself. Yet all the time he still feels that he is the real antithesis of Wagner, the man chosen to conquer Wagner from within, so to speak.

The Case of Wagner opens with a paean of praise for Bizet's *Carmen*.[5] We recognize no less than Nietzsche this opera's unique qualities. It is the happiest of blends – a natural melodiousness free of any sense of intellectual strain and swagger, artless yet artful in its limpidity, while its sprightliness and its formal perfection make it a wonderful evocation of the Mediterranean scene.

But by lauding the Spanish world of *Carmen* at the expense of the German world of Wagner, Nietzsche is comparing unlike things. Should one play off one nation, one race against another, when each has its own God-given characteristics? One wonders whether Nietzsche was really a German. And as for Bizet, he had a completely different view of Wagner from Nietzsche, bowing to his immeasurable greatness as willingly as did Verdi – whom some also try to play off against Wagner.

On a closer view, however, does Nietzsche's recourse to *Carmen* not begin to look like an exaggerated act of self-denial? Is it not an act of weariness on the part of a man who is desperately seeking a haven of safety and repose – not the safety of great art but a humbler, more easily accessible resting-place in the Mediterranean world? Is setting *Carmen* alongside the gigantic figure of Wagner not itself an act of decadence? Like any representative of decadence, when Nietzsche talks about *Carmen*, or any other subject, he talks too much about himself. His tastes are of little interest to us. What do we care if he suddenly found northern Europe too cold, too grey, and pined for the lighthearted southern pleasures of the dance? And all this in a tone which leaves no doubt that he is in earnest. But although he may take himself seriously, we can not. And although he jests at Wagner's expense, we see little to jest about.

That is not to say that *The Case of Wagner*, particularly its style and tone, had no impact. Nietzsche is now a completely different writer from the days of *Richard Wagner in Bayreuth*. He has learned to rid himself, *qua* writer, of Wagnerian influences and find his real self, setting out his thoughts boldly, clearly and with a sure hand. With deadly accuracy he captures the semi-ironic tone of the pseudo-intellectual and the mood of the modern man in the street. Then there is that slight but pervasive air of superiority and arrogance which the hundred-and-one little Nietzsches in our boulevard cafés have learned to imitate. What virtuosity of language, what wealth of allusion! And how fortunate that the target was the great Wagner! It is the mark of a poor lawyer to draw comparisons between things which have nothing in common – like Bizet and Wagner. One might as well compare a Strauss waltz with a Bach fugue. Yet how he lusts after spectacle and success! In this he is fully Wagner's equal. Did people not realize this? Why did they not fight against the effects of Nietzsche, which are at least as pernicious as those of Wagner and just as much the work of a seducer?

As I said above, through being aware of his own decadence, Nietzsche believed himself superior to Wagner, who was not aware of it. He described the chill wind of this awareness as the element that gave him the courage to confront himself with all the rigour and determination that he could command. This in turn, he said, heightened his perception of 'the most difficult and invidious kind of connection to draw, and where the greatest number of mistakes are made – the connection between the word and its author, between the deed and the doer, between the ideal and him who seeks it'. Thus: 'A desire for a stronger faith does not prove the presence of a stronger faith – rather the reverse'. To which one might retort: A desire for honesty and rigour does not prove the presence of these virtues – rather the reverse.

Stimulating as it was, the biological concept of the development and decay of spiritual and intellectual life also harboured certain dangers. It was a methodology with the disadvantages inherent in any methodology. So, in Nietzsche's own cryptic spirit, we may pose the question: Can such a methodology not be equally used in order to *escape* from the greatness of art, the greatness of a deed, the greatness of ideals? Is it not reasonable to ask what moves lay behind his passionate crusade to 'destroy all idols'? How different was Goethe, who, no stranger to the need for rejection, became ill-humoured when forced to do so, treating it as an unwelcome intrusion, on which he refused to spend a moment longer than was necessary! Nietzsche, by contrast, went out of his way to find things to spurn and to reject. It quickened his pulse. Not for nothing is he known as the inventor of the 'thrill of rejection'. To him the act of repudiation was a positive act, even a productive one, and the 'destruction of idols', as he called it – which did not stop short even at Christianity – was nothing less than an act of heroism.

Let there be no misunderstanding about this. I understand full well why this man, this particular man, with his absolute, unwavering honesty – towards himself no less than towards others – has become Europe's man of destiny. And I have not the slightest intention of belittling the tragic importance of his role. But as one who could see nothing around him save the manifestations of decadence, he is yesterday's man, out of date, overtaken by events. Above all, when he repudiates merely because, as in *The Case of Wagner*, he is being forced to repudiate himself, he ceases to interest us.

What does interest us, however, is: what was it in him that allowed him to repudiate himself in this way? The answer seems to lie in the observation that, side by side with his artistic temperament and his striving for effect there was still an element of indestructible rationalism in his make-up. The tendency to detached self-analysis, to challenging his own principles and actions, which appears in the later Nietzsche, may have been in him from the beginning. Indeed, may not the dualism of dedication to art on the one hand and sceptical rationalism on the other be a characteristic of his personality in general? May not the figure of Socrates, against whom he had launched that remarkable attack in the name of art in *The Birth of Tragedy* at the beginning of his career, actually represent one side of his nature? At that time the two sides were evenly balanced – the tragic work of art against the Socratic spirit of enquiry – and his dualism openly exposed. But the balance was subsequently destroyed. In his early days he sought to suppress the Socratic element in himself with Wagner's help; later he used Socrates in order to overcome the 'Wagnerian' in him, to help him put Wagner out of his mind. That he was at odds with himself, unable to come to terms with himself, is the surest mark of decadence.

Characteristic of all Nietzsche's writing on aesthetic matters is his concern not with art itself but with the emotions that it arouses in him, and it is these emotions that he sets out to analyse. He thus turns his mind increasingly to what lies behind the work of art, which naturally leads him to the mind of the artist. He announced that his *magnum opus* was to be called *The Physiology of Art*. What, we may ask, has physiology to do with art? Yet here too the world has come to understand Nietzsche all too clearly. For to trace art back to a series of biological, psychological, sexual and other similar sources, and 'explain' it by reference to these sources, is to reduce art to that which it is not.

Nevertheless art, i.e. the existence of the work of art, does have something to do with the artist's relationship to the world. Which leads us to the essential difference between Nietzsche and Wagner. An artist's attitude to the world will always differ from that of a philosopher. The artist is a man of action, bound to his immediate environment, the here and now, like any man with an activity to perform. On each occasion it is a case of '*Hic Rhodos, hic salta*'. He has to take circumstances into account, and the paths open to him, as to anyone contemplating an action, are limited. A true artist is one who is deeply conscious of the action-character of his activity. 'Artist,' demanded Goethe, '– work, don't talk'.[6]

The philosopher, on the other hand, is denied the opportunity of making a direct and immediate impact. He cannot make pronouncements on his own account but basically only reflect on the nature and activities of others, on the world in action. His influence is indirect. But the scope of this influence, in return, is immeasurably greater. To compensate him for his inability to perform a physical act of his own, so to speak, the winds carry his thoughts to far more distant places. He does not concern himself with the present; instead, he directs his attention to the past, to the future, to all other ages. As an observer, watching from without, he cannot influence the course of events. But he can survey them from on high. He is versatile. 'We may not have the greatness that goes with one-sidedness,' he says, 'but at least we do not have the one-sidedness that goes with greatness.'

There is a profound distinction to be drawn between thinking and living – of which latter art is part. The artist must strive to ensure that the act of creation does not become confused with the mere arrogant expression of opinion, or the created work, the product of responsible activity, be equated with arbitrary philosophical discussion. This is a distinction which becomes blurred to the philosopher, for he, in contrast to the artist, who experiences a fresh liberation with each new work he creates, is constantly forced back upon himself by the nature of his activity: his subject matter is the infinite, and his work can never be brought to a conclusion.

But the philosopher is exposed to the danger of seeking to claim a necessity for a virtue, to turn his incapacity into an advantage. It is no coincidence that it should be Nietzsche, the thinker, the philosopher, who first identified this situation, for he experienced it in the depths of his own being. In a moment of bitter self-analysis he wrote:

> I am only a word-maker.
> Who cares about words!
> Who cares about me!

When Wagner rejected something – and he rejected a great deal, and frequently – it was always in the name of the present. When Nietzsche rejected something – even when he believed he was making the same point – it was as a moralist holding up a mirror to mankind, at best in the name of a distant, all-too-distant future. In this sense he was right to call Wagner 'his great misapprehension'. For the struggle against the *cognoscenti* in Germany which brought Wagner and the young Nietzsche together, and which they waged side by side, was launched from two totally different positions. Nietzsche's feeling that they were making common cause – how far Wagner shared this feeling, we do not know – was in fact mere self-deception. The difference showed itself above all, however, in their relationship to art.

It is well known how decisive a role art played in Nietzsche's thought from the very beginning. Yet those of us who are concerned for the interests of art feel compelled to question his particular conception of art – indeed, to question whether he was capable of understanding art as it really is. I have already mentioned that his temperament and his disposition gave him a special relationship to music, although the great composers left him cold (this is not compensated by the fact that he made many telling observations on lesser figures). His spiteful description of Brahms as emanating the 'melancholy of impotence' seems, when one first hears it, to strike the nail on the head, like many of his formulations. But he allowed it – leaving aside the personal background – to obstruct any chance there might have been that he would come to appreciate the true greatness of Brahms. His above remark on Chopin belongs in the same context. He is susceptible to excellence on a small, but not on a large, scale, responsive to nuances but not to life in its fullness and wholeness.

Nor was this a characteristic limited to music. The greatest German lyric poet, in Nietzsche's eyes, was not Goethe or Hölderlin but Heine. He considered Roman poets and Roman stylists superior to Greek, while his grasp of the visual arts can only be described as pitiful. This did not prevent him from constantly striving to arrive at a definition and justification of art. But this justification betrays his true outlook on art. 'Art is exaltation,' he writes, 'and must be so. Art can only be conceived and born in a moment of euphoria and abundance of emotion'. The artist is 'Dionysian', he claims. But exuberance, intoxication, perfume, Chopin (as he saw him) are the *effects* of art, not art itself. And what this leads to becomes obvious in his relationship to Wagner. Once upon a time Wagner had represented art for him. When this pillar began to topple, it brought everything down with it. As he started to become suspicious of Wagner, so his suspicion soon extended to all artists.

The man who in his younger days had taken his bearings from art, both in his life and in his thought, now began to put the whole concept of art in question. This dualism, this thorn in his own flesh, was to have agonizing effects.

But this cut away the ground from his position vis-à-vis Wagner. Much as the reverse may seem to be the case, Nietzsche was far from being the ideal witness to testify against Wagner. So why did his anti-Wagner writings make such a tremendous impact? Why do we feel, reading his unbalanced, prejudiced outbursts, as though they correspond in some way to our own experience, and that there is a measure of truth in them? Why did *The Case of Wagner* have such an influence? Is there perhaps, we wonder, something in Wagner himself and in his works that actually supports such attacks and is thus grist to the mill of all those who have continued to strike an anti-Wagner stance down to this day?

Wagner is very different from other composers, especially from the other great composers. We are accustomed to the conception of the artist as a man who lives for and in his work, seeking to capture the richness of living reality and impose artistic form upon it. Wagner did not acknowledge this limitation. He sought to make an impact not only on art but on the world beyond, aimed to command the minds of men, to shatter and transform them, to redeem them from their callousness and brutishness, their egoism and isolation. Wagner the composer made enormous demands. But the demands of Wagner the man were still greater. One feels bound to ask: What was it that drove him on? Immensely gifted as he was, with all the natural power to express himself in and through his works, why did he feel impelled to make such demands? Are we perhaps confronting not only one of the most richly endowed composers of all time but also one of the most power-hungry?

At this point we must have regard to the circumstances of the age in which Wagner lived. Every artist is the product of the interaction between the Zeitgeist and himself. An age that favours and supports art will carry its artists along with it: they will not find it necessary to 'adjust' to it – i.e. in aesthetic terms, to over-assert themselves. Things are different, however, in an age – like the nineteenth century, and to an even greater extent the present day – which increasingly turns its back on art. Artists, so desperate to be accepted, come to believe that there is now only one way to overcome the apathy and insensitivity, even antagonism of those around them and ensure their survival. To speak, they conclude, is not enough. If they are to make themselves heard, they must shout.

We can see the effects of this on Brahms, Wagner's great contemporary and antithesis. He was no less an artistic nature than Wagner, no less sensitive to the spirit of his age. But he went a different way. Instead of turning outwards, like Wagner, he turned inwards. Coolly and deliberately he kept his mind on his art, ignoring anything that would have distracted his attention from it and convinced that in its final form it would stand as the expression of his experience. His works became ever more highly concentrated, ever more concise and more firmly compressed, whereas Wagner became ever more expansive. Yet the underlying reason is the same.

But Wagner's expansionist tendencies had consequences. The questions he asked required answers; the challenges he laid down demanded reactions. And so the 'Wagnerites' came into existence.

As far as I know, there have never been 'Bachians' or 'Beethovenians', and if one talked of 'Brahmsians', then only as opponents of the 'Wagnerites'. These latter were at their most numerous at the end of the nineteenth century, when the dominion of Wagner's music was at its height. Since that time their numbers have been steadily declining but they have by no means died out. As the example of Nietzsche shows, those who joined their ranks were often far from being the basest of men. But I am not concerned with individuals. What I mean is a particular state of mind, as characteristic of Wagner himself as of 'Wagnerites'. So what is a Wagnerite?

He is a person who has taken up his position not outside Wagner's work but in the middle of it, having been unable to retain his spiritual freedom and independence in the face of this music, to which he has surrendered himself body and soul. As most of the literature on Wagner shows, such a man has little chance of converting others to the Master's cause; on the contrary, he is more likely to meet with opposition.

There are people who make Wagner himself responsible for this, laying most of the blame on his domineering personality and the autocratic nature of his writings. This may well apply to a number of his close supporters during his lifetime. His relationship to Nietzsche, as we have already seen, shows how prone he was to sacrifice everything and everybody to the furtherance of his own cause.

But this is by no means the end of the matter. The reason for the Wagnerite's unconditional self-abandonment, a virtual self-immolation, lies far more deeply embedded in Wagner's works than in his personality. A confrontation with these works is quite different from that with any other works of art. So immediate, so powerful, so vital is this confrontation that one can no longer talk about the impact of these works in the conventional sense. They have often been compared to the casting of a magic spell. Subject-matter, theatre and the insistent fervour of a music borne aloft by the passion of infinite yearning combine to make the submissive listener feel that he is experiencing a huge magnification of the real world. What has hitherto been called art seems by comparison to be mere play, fancy, somehow trivial. Only Wagner reveals the deadly seriousness of life in all its immensity and all its profundity.

Germany had already known a work that had had a similar impact to Wagner's music dramas – Goethe's *Werther*, the effects of which were incomparably greater than were to be expected from works of art. Young men throughout Germany and far beyond were overwhelmed by it, and a wave of lachrymose sentimentality spread across Europe, the consequence of this one novel. Men surrendered to its emotionality and imitated its hero's behaviour. It was like a sickness.[7]

The effect of Wagner's works on the Wagnerites was not dissimilar to that of *Werther* on its immediate public. In both cases it was the subject matter itself that made the impact, not the allegory or the imagery. But in the case of Wagner the pathological effect was to be longer-lasting. After *Werther* Goethe struck out in new directions, whereas Wagner, the true tragic artist – Goethe was not a writer of tragedy and had no desire to be – persisted in his chosen vein with an ever-rising intensity. In music, moreover, he possessed the means of enveloping his creation in a radiant, irresistible aura of reality and heightening the dramatic effect by the way the music penetrates the action. Each individual work is dominated by an atmosphere, a mood generated by the music in and for that work alone, maintained throughout from beginning to end and undisturbed by a single note, a single harmony that does not have its place in the world created by that work. The immediacy of this insidious musical appeal, sometimes enervating, sometimes destructive, ever straining to attain gigantic proportions, plays a large part in the impact made by Wagner's works.

Wagnerites are totally overwhelmed by this impact. One can hardly fail to recognize its pathological nature, or that those who have no intention of submitting to it are filled with resentment, even animosity. The perfect example of this reaction is the Nietzsche of *Richard Wagner in Bayreuth*, in which all the arguments, culminating in Nietzsche's agonizing over the justification of art, are a reflection of this situation.

The excesses, the tendency to drive everything to extremes, characteristic of Wagner's life, are equally typical of his works – and for the same reason: his era and the circumstances of his life compelled him to be thus. In his music too he felt forced to repeat everything twice or three times in order to make sure that his listeners understood him. It was the tribute exacted from him by the age – but it no way detracted from the wealth of his imagination or deprived his works of any of their inner strength. There is one person, however, who can never fall victim to what I have called the pathological effect of the work of art, the effect that spawns 'Wagnerites'. That person is the creator of the work himself. At the time of *Werther* Goethe was the only man who seemed unaffected by his work. The remarks that he later addressed to the readers of his novel were to have ended with the words: 'Now be a man and follow not my path.'[8]

With Wagner it is the same. The young Nietzsche expressed his admiration and amazement that one and the same composer could write two so completely different works as *Tristan und Isolde* and *Die Meistersinger* one immediately after the other. How was it possible, he wondered, for the man who at one moment was submerged in the frightening depths of the most terrible tragedy to emerge the very next moment into a bright, positive world of optimism and serenity. Wagner's strength was like Goethe's. By the act of creation, by giving rounded living form to his work, he liberated himself from the subject-matter. The creator of these mighty works is not their prisoner. Wagner is not a Wagnerite. He has established the necessary distance between himself and his works for him to be able to view them as entities. And this he can do because – this is the crux of the matter – he is an artist. The work of art becomes an image, a metaphor, and its creator shows us the way in which it can become for us what he intended it to become.

As soon as we embark upon this road, however, a remarkable change seems to come over us. The heaviness, the oppressiveness, the unremitting seriousness, the sense of endless yearning, that eerie experience of a continuously expanding and intensifying universe – all this gradually recedes and ultimately vanishes altogether. The smouldering sensuousness of the music, so characteristic of Wagner's 'style', seems to lose its effect. We suddenly notice how varied are the forms in which this sensuousness is expressed, how immediately it emerges from the individual dramatic situation, and in particualr how different the expression of sensuous and erotic impulses is in Wagner from what we find in his successors or elsewhere in modern music – the French impressionist composers, for example. When emotions are aroused, it is never for their own sake, in a sterile spirit of self-gratification, but with a goal in view, a promise of fulfilment. No longer are we caught up in the attractions of the moment but can see the whole course of the action

before us and live it out as it unfurls. Not only do we share
Tristan's sufferings as though they were our own, we also feel
their necessity, feel that they are leading Tristan, and us, to a
process of purification through which we can achieve our destiny. The fulfilment of the tragedy of the ill-starred lovers
acquires for us a completely new dimension.

It is therefore our obligation, as listeners, to revise our attitude
towards Wagner. Instead of asking whether his works will live
up to our demands, we should be seeking to change ourselves
and our attitudes so that we can live up to the demands of his
works.

But is an artist entitled to make such demands? An artist of
decadence is a subjectivist. He is not concerned with things as
they are but with how he relates to them. Indeed, this is the
only way he can perceive them. Of vital importance to him is
that he perpetually feels attracted to things, does not become
bored. His taste and his moods mean more to him than all the
realities in the world. At the same time one must emphasize
that a real work of art makes its own demands: it requires the
public to be worthy of it. 'A work of art is like a king,' said
Schopenhauer. 'One has to wait until one feels addressed.'[9] A
work of art – and the greater the work, the truer this becomes
– has to be accepted for what it is. One can no more ask it to
be something else than one can ask an apple-tree to produce
pears.

Here we must say a few words on the moot question of
what art actually is. There are people who regard Nietzsche, for
example, as an artist. The work of art is not merely emotion,
passion, exuberance, an act of love, as Nietzsche thought. It is
all of these things, but it is also something more – an organism.
What does this mean? We are ourselves organisms and have a
particular affinity with everything organic. In one way or
another every work of art forms part of the organic life of the
universe. Life and art constitute a single entity. Our awareness
of this organic quality exists side by side with our expressive
faculties, our moods and our human emotions, all of which it
subtly and imperceptibly permeates (this has nothing to do
with what philosophers call aesthetic pleasure. It may have an
elevating or liberating effect but its nature is purely instinctive).

Nowadays, however, the work of art has become confused
with the moods and emotions that it evokes in us. Nietzsche
too made this error, which is why he failed to understand that
the artist has the will and the capacity to identify himself with

his work *while yet remaining himself.* Only thus can we explain how the artist has the strength to conjure up from his mind a series of totally different images, totally different worlds. Wagner's faith in the particular image that he is creating remains total to the point of self-denial, yet he knows that it is only an image, only part of the world, the world viewed only from one angle. He knows that the mystery of the world cannot be unravelled, cannot be expressed in terms of a single common denominator, as a philosopher like Nietzsche would have us believe.

As we know from Nietzsche's own testimony, his final break with Wagner came as a result of what he called Wagner's 'genuflection before the Cross', that is, the Christian content of *Parsifal*. Had he forgotten about *Tannhäuser* and *Lohengrin*? Did he believe that Wagner was only to be identified with his Siegfried? How gross was the rationalist's misunderstanding of the artist! Does not each of Wagner's works embody a different philosophy of life? The secular Germanic world of Siegfried, the Christian world of Parsifal, the doom-laden Tristan, the extrovert Mastersingers, Tannhäuser's dualism, Lohengrin's monism – where is the true Wagner? What did the creator of all these works really believe – for he must have had beliefs of his own? – The works are images – each is a metaphor, a parable. They are real, yet not real. The artist is here more profound than the philosopher.

Today people have lost all sense of the meaning of such parables, just as they have largely forgotten how to use the power that would lead them to this meaning, namely, the power of the imagination. Our intellectualized modern-day world, governed by a determined pragmatism, leaves little room for parables. It is, therefore, particularly significant that recent psychoanalytical research has produced evidence to show the importance of the function of this so neglected faculty of imagination. Experiments have revealed the existence in the human unconscious of primeval, elemental images which emerge at particular moments such as dreams. A new understanding of the nature and function of imagery is beginning to dawn, stimulated by science – which people today seem more ready to believe, although in our case its procedures are circuitous.

Wagner's works, every one of them, are primeval parables of this kind – *Ur*-myths. Through his unique combination of temperament and talent he summons them up not only from his own personal unconscious but from the collective unconscious of the whole German people, even of the whole of European civilization, and lays them out before us. We, however, in our superior wisdom, prisoners of the superficial everyday world, refuse to recognize ourselves in the mirror that he holds up to us.

But a myth, a parable is at the same time an artistic creation. And here we face a difficulty. A work of art must be capable of being perceived as an entity, integral, simple. All true art is simple. The archetypal Wagnerite, however, while succumbing to the effect of the whole, falls victim to one or other of its parts. He overestimates the libretto, the underlying philosophy, or, most frequently, the music, and thus renders himself incapable of countering the most fundamental and most widely-heard criticism of Wagner, *viz.* that his works are a piecemeal assemblage of different elements.

If, however, Wagner's works are integral and simple, it must be possible to find an integral and simple term to apply to them. That word is poetic. Wagner is a Poet, at all times and in all places, and he remains a Poet in spite of the variety of the media he employs. He is a Poet when he composes music – and even when he adds stage directions. A particularly striking example of the poetic effect he achieves comes in Act One of *Tannhäuser*, at the moment when, as Tannhäuser invokes the Virgin Mary, the Venusberg vanishes and the countryside around the Wartburg appears. The music at this point is hardly memorable – an insignificant tune sung by the Shepherd Boy, broken into by a characterless ritornello on the cor anglais. On the stage, a set – which consists, after all, merely of cardboard and canvas. Yet it is as though we had never seen so beautiful a May morning, as though God's world had never appeared so glorious. The reason is psychological: we experience the scene through the consciousness of Tannhäuser. And his cry 'Thanks to Thee, Almighty, great are the wonders of Thy grace!' must be one of the greatest moments in the whole of literature. What other name can one give to a man capable of producing such an effect than that of Poet, even when, as here, the centre of attention is not poetry, or music, but just a simple scene-change?

This is only one example among many. Using the most varied ways and means, now this technique, now another, Wagner constantly aims at direct poetic effect. No-one ever put the theatre to his own purpose in such a multitude of different ways. Wagner is the king of theatre, even the God of theatre. He plays on it like an instrument. Is that a shortcoming? Or something to disparage? Shakespeare was theatre and little else, yet no-one thinks to turn that against him. But with Wagner, and only with Wagner, the word 'theatre' has acquired an unpleasant flavour.

One reason for this is a matter which I must mention in conclusion, a matter which is always calculated to fan the flames of the argument that rages round the alleged dominance of an 'instinct for theatricality' in Wagner. This is the question of performance.

Let me first interject a personal experience. I was relatively late getting to know Wagner's music, but the closer I studied his works, the more mysterious became his hold over me. I was then given my first ticket for a performance of the complete *Ring* cycle in Munich, where there was an outstanding cast of singers. The conductor was Franz Fischer, and everything augured well. Yet as I well remember, although I had looked forward to the occasion with great excitement, it left me with a profound sense of disappointment. I could not understand what had happened. When I had studied the piano score, I had felt elated, full of enthusiasm, in a seventh heaven of delight; now I could barely recognize what I was listening to. All that I knew seemed to have disappeared, leaving an empty, showy, exaggerated theatricality. Even the few moments of orchestral beauty could not outweigh the overall impression of something fundamentally false. The experience 'cured' me of Wagner for many years afterwards.

Some considerable time later I again found myself at a performance of one of the *Ring* dramas in a leading German opera house. Again there were singers of repute and a well-known conductor. The impression, I must confess, was almost exactly the same. By the end of the first act I had to admit to myself that in the face of what I had just heard, Wagner's most virulent antagonists were absolutely right – it was a piece of shallow, meretricious, artificial theatre, and nothing more. Yet – and this was the worst aspect of the situation – it was not even what one could call a bad performance. Indeed, it was thoroughly well-organized, as far as the blending of the individual elements was concerned. But audiences have no idea how remote such a reading is from the original. They accept it without demur, as they are also accustomed to accepting distorted performances of Beethoven symphonies and other works without complaint.

What is lacking in such performances? Wagner once said that the primary concern of singers, players, producers, stage designers and all the others must be for the clarity of the performance – clarity of both external and internal action: once this clarity had been achieved, so-called expressiveness would follow of its own accord.

The clarity that Wagner here deliberately opposes to 'expressiveness', theatrical effect, is not easy to accomplish, in the first place for external reasons. The words are hard to follow, not least because of the size of the orchestra. But if the listener is to enjoy and absorb the work to the full, he *must* follow them – every one of them. To help solve this problem he included in his design for the Bayreuth Festspielhaus the well-known canopy above the orchestra, albeit at the cost of part of the richness of the orchestral timbre. But this was only a solution for Bayreuth. In general the only answer appears to be for the listener to have mastered the words to the point where he almost knows them by heart, if he is to comprehend the works in their fullness – and this is no modest demand for a composer to make of his listeners.

But there are also other factors that contrive to hinder the creation of that clarity, that total unity of experience, which Wagner sought. In practical terms the individual elements of the *Gesamtkunstwerk* have a persistent tendency towards independence. The singers seek to dominate the musical proceedings, an over-prominent orchestra may drown the singers, the producer may thrust himself into the limelight at the expense of the music, the designer, the maître de ballet – are all preoccupied with their own area of activity and all insist on their share of attention, leaving the final result, the purpose of the whole exercise, more or less to chance. And every participant in the enterprise has as his goal the creation of what the professionals call 'theatrical effect'. The interests of theatre come to exert a fatal influence over the dramatist's works; the urge to overstatement and the demand for effect at all costs destroy the poet's work.

Wagner feared, even foresaw, just such a fate as this for performances of his works, and throughout his life he was at pains to provide principles and instructions which would establish a style of performance. This was one of the driving forces behind his foundation of the Bayreuth Festspielhaus, a place where works that required such a high degree of co-operation between those involved in them could be nurtured and brought to fruition with the requisite practical objectivity and tenacity of purpose, thereby establishing a tradition of performance.

But tradition is a strange thing. Experience shows that it

begins to crumble as early as the second generation. This is not surprising. Unless the essential meaning of a work, its inner substance, is not passed on together with external features like style of performance, that inner substance will quickly become meaningless and irrelevant. But it is not possible to pass on this inner meaning directly – it can only be done *via* performers of like mind and spirit. And such performers cannot be reared or cultivated – they just have to be there, available. Their presence is always a stroke of fortune, and one cannot anticipate it, or depend on it. Yet there is no substitute for it.

The ways in which tradition is handed down follow much the same path. Nuances of emotion which were initially conveyed mutedly, gently, with sensitive restraint, become increasingly coarse and unrefined as time goes on. A slight easing of the tempo, for instance, becomes a massive ritardando, and gently dwelling on individual notes is turned into a succession of fermatas. It is a law of traditions that the longer they last, the more exaggerated their expression of emotion becomes.

This is a special danger in the case of Wagner, in whom the expression of emotion already seems to be stretched to the limits of intensity and to have acquired superhuman proportions. It is only a short step from the intensely passionate to the grotesque and the ludicrous. Even the slightest of exaggerations can be fatal. As far as the gestures, the action is concerned, whether on the stage or in the music, Wagner must be performed as simply and straightforwardly as possible – all the traditions that can genuinely be traced directly back to him have proven this time and again. But modern productions have ignored it. Wagner the dramatist, Wagner the poet has become the victim of the medium through which he communicates and on which he is dependent – the theatre. In the orchestral playing as in the singing, in the gestures as in the expression of emotion, we have lost the feeling for simplicity, for directness, for what is appropriate and necessary.

In the light of this we can see how tragically right Nietzsche was when he talked of 'Wagner the play-actor'. And his talk of Wagner the 'Great Seducer', Wagner the dissembler and imposter, finds fertile soil on which to settle, once it has been prepared by attitudes and productions of the kind I have described.

To conclude. In principle our relationship today to the works of Wagner has not advanced beyond the position adopted by Nietzsche over half a century ago. He embodies our two basic responses – on the one hand an unconditional surrender to Wagner's art, a declaration of total devotion, on the other hand a no less radical repudiation of everything he stands for, an expression of antipathy and deep distaste. But like so many, Nietzsche allowed himself to become bogged down in arguments relating to details of content. We must take the argument beyond this and discuss it in terms of the real Wagner, Wagner the poet, the dramatist, the composer – in short, of Wagner the artist. Only in this way shall we be able to discover a new and genuinely productive relationship to his works. And only then shall we become aware who this artist really was.

9   Brahms

One reason why The Brahms Society decided to accept the invitation from The Society of the Friends of Music to transfer the celebration of the centennial of Brahms' birth to Vienna, lies in the nature of his relationship to that city. For Brahms, as for Beethoven, Vienna became a second home, offering him the atmosphere and the stimuli which his North German temperament, highly vulnerable in its amalgam of a taciturn masculinity and an excessive sensitivity, so desperately needed.

But there is also another reason why we, as Germans, chose Vienna for our celebrations. We should not forget, either in Germany or in Austria – and regardless of what our political masters think – that in cultural terms we inhabit one and the same world, and that the Viennese classical composers are also German classical composers. Nowhere is the sense of unity and common purpose more strongly felt than here. And there is every justification for considering Brahms to be the last of these Classical 'Viennese' German composers.

Brahms' music succeeded in establishing itself from the moment of its first publication – that is to say, irrespective of objective analysis and often disparaging criticism, it immediately became a force to be reckoned with. We too, assembled here today in his name, are still under its spell, a spell evident and undeniable yet not so easy to explain. If, for instance, we look at his position in the history of music, we can hardly deny that those who maintain that he in fact contributed nothing new to music are right. And if one views history in terms of progress and development, it is hard to see how one can admit him to the ranks of the great masters at all. Moreover the immediate impact of his works was by no means remarkable, and throughout his life he stood in the shadow of Wagner. Later others appeared – Bruckner, Richard Strauss – who also, in their turn, pushed Brahms into second place.

Nevertheless, if we ask ourselves today who was the last

German composer to leave an indelible mark on the world of music, the answer would have to be – if we exclude the incomparable figure of Wagner – Brahms. In the English-speaking world, in America no less than in Northern Europe, he is one of the best known and most frequently performed of all composers, regarded as the last great representative of nineteenth-century German music. In France and Italy too people are coming to appreciate his classical qualities and his significance. Indeed, apart from the internationally-minded and internationally successful Richard Strauss, no German composer who came after him – not his contemporary Bruckner, not Pfitzner, not Reger – has succeeded to such an extent in making himself known beyond the frontiers of his native country.

Another thing strikes us when we look at the fate of Brahms' music. Its impact and importance are still growing – more accurately, has started to grow again. I well remember, when I was setting out on my career some twenty years ago, how the Berlin critics often superciliously dismissed it. I particularly recall reading in a not uninfluential paper that there was nothing tragic about Brahms' Tragic Overture save the composer's complete and utter incompetence. One does not read remarks like that today.

More important is the fact that responsible people's attitudes to Brahms are changing. It is an interesting situation. When Brahms' music was first published, the German middle classes took it to their hearts as though it had been written with them in mind. His songs were seen as the successors to those of Schumann, and his orchestral music as consolidating the great classical tradition, especially that of Beethoven. There was less desire at this time for novelty, and the notion of 'progress' as the aim of art – a notion which today, incidentally, seems to have faded away yet again – had not yet been born. It was only later, as this notion increasingly took hold of the minds of the general public, as the victory of Wagner's music became complete at the end of the nineteenth century, and as figures such as Richard Strauss began to appear, that Brahms was finally banished to the background. He became regarded in many circles as *passé*, reactionary, of no relevance for the future, and was thrown on to the scrap heap. But as time went on, people began to observe, to their astonishment, that whereas most of the modern 'music of the future', loudly trumpeted and lavishly promoted, began to collect dust in a remarkably short time, the tranquil music of Brahms, dismissed as way behind the times, not only retained its pristine vigour undiminished but even began to shine forth with a new radiance.

There has been much talk in modern aesthetics of the concept of 'objectivity', 'factuality'. The avant-garde coined the slogan 'New Objectivity'[1] – the only thing new about which was that the word Objectivity regained some of its former substance and meaning. For in itself, of course, objectivity is neither old nor new but a precondition for any kind of substantial achievement, whatever its nature.

Let us look at the word itself. 'Objectivity' denotes a concentration on 'objects' as such, which implies the exclusion of influences which lie outside those objects, such as the trends and fashions of the moment. Here our 'New Objectivity' shows itself to be the very opposite of what it claims to be. In the realm of music, objectivity must imply clear and precise understanding of what makes music into an art. This happens when the logic of a sequence of spiritual events become equated with the logic of a sequence of musical events, in other words, when the spiritual and the musical fuse so completely that there is no way they can be separated, from whatever side one approaches them.

In this sense I would call Brahms the 'objective' composer *par excellence*. In an age obsessed with the creation of 'effect' through the build-up of tension, through the instrumentation, through drawing on the forces of nature etc. – when composers, great and small alike, seized every available opportunity to achieve such 'effects', Brahms looked studiously in the opposite direction. He uses the orchestra with a restraint derived from the classical composers, ignoring the developments which came with Wagner and which exercised such a fascination on his contemporaries. He keeps to his concise, small-scale forms – indeed, the older he became, the simpler, the more compact, the more relaxed and anti-theatrical became the spiritual content of these works, for all their profundity and inner strength. They are controlled by a strict inner logic such as is found only in the very greatest. The artistic utterance says no more than the object – i.e. the world embodied by the work in question – requires. All alien thoughts are dismissed, all the cheap attractions of what is referred to as 'a wealth of inventiveness' – in effect a euphemism for an inadequate power of concentration – are spurned. In return, what Brahms says, he says clearly, fully and consistently – because he has something to say. What a contrast to most of those around him and to most of what has been written since his time!

When we therefore consider Brahms' *oeuvre* as a whole – the same applies to his life, if we view it in the proper light – we might describe it as being inspired by a 'passionate objectivity'. It was this objectivity that enabled him to remain true to himself in an age of incipient decay and disintegration. His contemporaries did not make it easy for him to do so; diffident and reserved by nature, the only way he found he could counter offensive allegations was often by offensive behaviour of his own. His boorishness became proverbial, as inordinate as its cause was deep-seated, namely, a boundless desire for freedom and independence. Yet at the same time he was always receptive to the joys of honest conviviality and to the benefits that the company of genuine friends could bring.

The fact that those around him often spoke of his eccentricities and his shameless egoism has its roots in the deep contempt that he felt in later years for the world and his fellow-men – those, that is, involved in 'running' the world. At the same time he realized, as an artist, that he could not do without them in the practical affairs of everyday life. So on occasions when he did not resort to scorn and rudeness, he could always call on a sarcastic wit to deal with the occasion – though those at whom this wit was aimed often realized only later, or not at all, how deep it went. There are numerous anecdotes about him, especially from Vienna, and it would be worth while making a collection of them, arranged according to the issues which we still find relevant today. We would then realize what most of his contemporaries did not, and could not, realize, namely, how superior he was, in mind and spirit, to those of his age. True, he did not have the explosive, overwhelming personal power of Wagner. But his clarity of vision and understanding, his sense of responsibility towards life, were no less pronounced for that, and an apparently casual remark could reveal a wealth of insights.

There are many examples of this. Richard Strauss related how, when he showed Brahms his early Symphony in F minor, Brahms said: 'All this contrapuntal to-ing and fro-ing between subjects and bits of subjects in order to keep the thread of the music intact is no good. Far more useful and more necessary – and more difficult too – is to learn how to write a simple eight-bar phrase'. As I recall, Strauss told this story without comment, and Brahms could not, of course, have foreseen the enormous development that was to take place in Strauss' music. But leaving this aside – did he not put his finger on one of the greatest dangers threatening the whole subsequent development of music? The whole subject of Brahms and his contemporaries, I would note in passing, offers a wealth of interesting material. I am full of admiration for his frankness and honesty towards those around him. When any question was put to him, his sense of responsibility would not allow him to give evasive answers or take refuge in soft-sounding phrases. But this directness also gained him his most powerful and most dogged opponents, making one wonder whether it was really necessary for him to be as brutally frank as he was about, say, Nietzsche or Hugo Wolf.[2]

Brahms' distaste for external show, his complete and utter lack of vanity, together with the 'passionate objectivity' about which I spoke a moment ago, were equally characteristic of his daily life. His need for independence and his cast-iron determination not to allow himself to be disturbed by trivial interruptions, led to his living an unobtrusive, almost anonymous life, to the point of self-caricature, where he indulged in semi-ironic, semi-sceptical orgies of self-denigration. Such behaviour was, of course, frequently misunderstood. Some really believed him when he declared that he had never really enjoyed any of his works – as though, in that case, he could ever have written them! And they took it at face value when he pretended to compare his position in the history of music to that of Cherubini. His habit of asking close friends, especially women, like Clara Schumann and Elisabeth von Herzogenberg, for their opinion of his works and suggestions for alterations in them, belongs to the same context. When, misreading the situation, they were naive enough to offer him such suggestions, they were surprised to find that they were not taken seriously.

In fact he was loath to talk about his works at any time. Like all truly objective artists he was fully aware of the distinction between the real creative act that manifests itself in the work of art itself and the sophisticated theorizing about it which was just beginning to become fashionable in his day, and which has since become such an intolerable feature of our own oh-so-knowledgeable age. Particularly in the last years of his life he lived with the future, with eternity, in mind. We know from accounts of his dealings with Hans von Bülow how relatively unimportant he considered it whether his works were performed or not, and if so, then how they were performed. During the last years of his life, I was told, he went so far as to perform his late chamber music, such as the two clarinet sonatas and the Trio for clarinet, cello and piano, without regard for clarity or accuracy – badly, in other words – as though he were playing merely for his own amusement. The every-day world ceased to matter and intruded less and less upon his consciousness.

Brahms belongs to that race of Germanic musical giants which began with Bach and Handel and continued with Beethoven. He combined immense physical strength with the utmost sensitivity and gentleness. Both in build and in character he was of Nordic stock – I like to see him as a descendant of those old Dutch or German painters like van Eyck and Rembrandt, whose works combine a warmth and intensity of imagination with a fearful concentration of power and a wonderful sense of form. This affinity with the spiritual world of the Old German Masters is particularly prominent in his great sets of variations. His creative powers were enormous, and his sense of form reveals itself in everything of his that has survived, from the briefest of letters down to his songs and symphonies.

Moreover it is a peculiarly German kind of form, there not for its own sake but for that of the musical substance, a remarkable fusion of an intense, highly-charged subject matter with a form of remarkable equanimity and clarity. He inhabits a world of fantasy and demonic abandon – yet a world at the same time held togther in a taut organic structure. If ever there was a perfect composer to give the lie to the charge frequently levelled at the Germans that their music is rough hewn and incapable of being moulded into Classical forms, it is Brahms.

Histories of music usually state that Brahms did not undergo a process of musical development like Beethoven or Wagner. This is, of course, untrue. His development was as marked and as natural as that of any other great composer but his personality and the nature of the task that he had been predestined to undertake directed his development along different paths. Unlike Beethoven and Wagner he did not conquer new territories, because as he saw it, there were no such territories left. His development took the form of intensification, not expansion. The older he grew, the more compact and concise his works became, the simpler and more direct the emotions he expressed. He is living proof that there is a mode of evolution characterized not by an increasing complexity but by an increasing simplicity. Like Beethoven, Brahms constantly sought to concentrate a subject-matter of overwhelming power into the simplest and most succinct form possible, not – as the general tendency later became – to take a modest content and shape it into an inflated and apparently chaotic structure.

Here, unexpectedly, Brahms acquires a particular relevance for the present day. He was the first to realize – without becoming a reactionary *laudator temporis acti* – that to see music, or any of the other arts, in terms of perpetual progress was an illusion. It is a realization that has been dawning on people again in recent times. Anticipating the contemporary situation, Brahms showed that it was possible to do other things in music than expand and magnify one's material *ad infinitum*. He has made us aware that what appeared to be old and familiar can yet show us paths that lead to the new and unfamiliar, and that by pausing to look around us and retracing our steps across well-known territory, we can find a field of activity for the present and a challenge for the future.

There is another, more specific sense in which Brahms is of importance to us today. It is what I would define as his popular affiliation – a quality not greatly prized in recent decades but one to which we are today becoming more receptive. By this term I do not just mean that Brahms was 'a child of the people'. He was that, but this is not important here. What I am thinking of is his power to make the great supra-personal concept of the people the source of his emotions, indeed of his whole existence. This faculty was present in him from the beginning but it became more prominent as his life progressed. Side by side with his quartets and symphonies he wrote popular music such as Hungarian dances and gypsy songs; he was also a great lover and collector of German folksongs – one of his last works was an incomparable collection of settings of such songs.

But I have in mind something more specific than this. For Brahms, similar in this respect to his great predecessors, had the ability to write melodies which were unmistakeably his, down to the last detail, and which yet sounded like folksongs. Or, put the other way round, melodies that were genuine folk-songs yet composed by Brahms. With Mahler, for example, it was quite the reverse. Mahler's relationship to the folksong was that of a stranger, an outsider, a man who yearned to find refuge in it, a haven of peace for his restless spirit. Taking it over as it stood, he merely created synthetic folksongs.

Brahms, however, *was* the folk, *was* the folksong. He could not be otherwise, whether he was writing symphonies, quartets or songs. He could thus pour his whole personality into the space of two bars and at the same time retain his universal accessibility, composing modern, original music which still appealed to the common consciousness. Wagner and Bruckner possessed the same gift, and I have no hesitation in maintaining that this represents creativity at its highest and constitutes the mark of genius. Brahms achieved what so many contemporary wiseacres have time and again turned their backs on, namely, the mysterious synthesis of subjective personality and objective realization, of the apparent limitations of the individual vision and an unconditional surrender to those higher forces which unite the whole of mankind. This is the light in which we must see his Classical form: it is not something borrowed from elsewhere but the natural and necessary expression of his own nature. Classical form, its validity unquestioned and unqualified in time and place, is not, as earlier critics claimed, merely a 'formal' matter but an expression of nature herself. It is his union with nature that makes Brahms a Classic. And if we were to add that this union with nature is related to his identification with the spirit of the people, then . . . but this is not the place to go into the question of the genesis of Classical form – perhaps the most misunderstood chapter in the whole history of aesthetics.

The people, the folksong world to which Brahms belonged, was German. What he achieved, he achieved by virtue of being German – not by virtue of *wanting* to be German but of actually *being* German. He had no choice. And although he eagerly responded to stimuli from all over the non-German world, it was in terms of his German-ness that he came to understand and conquer this world. In its acerbity and its sweetness, its outward reticence and inner serenity, its exuberance of imagination and its nobility of discipline, his music is German. He was the last composer we have seen who demonstrated to the world the greatness of German music.

10 Bruckner

My justification for talking about Bruckner lies less in the fact that I happen at present to be President of the German Bruckner Society than in my lifelong association with Bruckner's works and the feelings they arouse in me. The first work I ever conducted – for better or for worse – was Bruckner's Ninth Symphony.[1] I was twenty at the time, and many are the occasions since then when I have acted as advocate for his music. There are various angles from which one can approach a man like Bruckner. My concern here will be with the fate of his music, in particular the errors and misconceptions to which it has been exposed.

Bruckner's magnificent works have become part and parcel of the life of Germans today. Maybe they owe this to their quality of timelessness, for they compel us to put on one side the historical methods which are like a millstone round our necks when we set about trying to evolve a direct relationship to the music of the past. Not that Bruckner was not a product of his age. But whereas his contemporaries Wagner and Brahms were responsible to a large degree for moulding and fashioning their age, the one striking out in new directions, the other consolidating the achievements of the past, Bruckner stood apart. He was not composing for the present but for eternity. As a result, he has become the most misunderstood of all the great composers.

He was different from his predecessors in all respects, starting with the course of his development. His career began only in middle-age, when others have a life's work behind them. Schubert and Mozart had already completed their careers when Bruckner was still at the stage of doing exercises in counterpoint. There have, of course, been composers who wrote great works in advanced years – of Haydn and Verdi we might say that in old age they were still young. But Bruckner is the only one we know who discovered his creative powers so late in life. How appropriate this seems when we come to consider the nature of his music!

Bruckner's personality presents something of an enigma. On the one hand he was the self-confident artist, the creator of works original down to their last detail; on the other hand he was a childlike nature, unsure of himself, an unworldly rustic, the man who once wrote to his Emperor simply to beg His Majesty to protect him against the attacks of a much-feared critic. How can we reconcile this with the principle of the unity of man and artist which the world's great artists all serve to exemplify?

The reception of his works underwent a similarly uneven, untypical, paradoxical fate. Controversial at the time they appeared and subjected to unparalleled attacks, they never enjoyed an unchallenged success. At the very beginning of his public career there was a misconception about his position in the conflict between 'drama-based' and 'absolute' music – between Wagner and Brahms – in which he was mistakenly taken to belong to the Wagnerian camp. There were reasons for this but in reality Bruckner was no less absolute a composer than Brahms. Nevertheless it was his opposition to Brahms – intensified by the activities of the so-called friends of both parties – that later set the seal on his position as far as the public was concerned.

We can never be too grateful to those of his contemporaries who took upon themselves the thankless task of bringing Bruckner's music to the attention of the public. How immense this task was, how wide the gulf that separated Bruckner's view of music from that which prevailed in Viennese cultural circles at the time, can be seen from a recent striking development. I am thinking here of the publication, forty years after Bruckner's death, of the original versions of the symphonies, which we owe to the selfless efforts of a number of scholars, most notably Robert Haas.[2]

During Bruckner's lifetime perceptive musicians like Franz Schalk and Ferdinand Löwe, his devoted pupils, considered it impossible to perform his works in their original form, despairing of being able to make them intelligible to audiences. Hence their revised versions, intended to bridge the gulf. How Bruckner himself viewed these revisions; to what extent he was involved in them, if at all; whether he merely put up with them or even protested against them: all these are questions that will probably remain for ever unanswered. Nor can we foretell what importance the publication – still in progress – of the original versions will acquire in the future. The struggle and ultimate success achieved by Bruckner's music had been on the basis of the revised versions known earlier but the original versions are highly revealing for our knowledge of his emotional development, his stylistic aims and his musical language. The differences lie partly in the orchestration, partly in the tempo markings and in both respects the original versions have a greater simplicity, a greater sense of unity and directness which seems to correspond more closely to the expansiveness of Bruckner's nature. In the many instances where the cuts have been restored, we feel a sense of greater organic cohesion, not only in the particular, from one bar to another, but in respect of the movement as a whole. The points at which these cuts had been most ruthlessly made – such as in the Finale of the Fifth Symphony, which used to be 122 bars shorter than now – are precisely the points where the greater power, clarity and effectiveness of the original version are undeniable. It is as though we were looking at this monumental Finale for the first time.

These different versions of Bruckner's symphonies present us with a highly unusual situation. Who else among the great composers do we find perpetually rewriting his works? Beethoven, we know, wrote slowly and laboriously but once the creative process was over, the work was finished. With Bruckner it is almost as though no work were ever quite finished, as though it were in the nature of this colossal music to strive ever onwards and upwards, never reaching final, definitive form.

The history of the reception of Bruckner's music is, as I said, unusual. Slowly but surely, under the baton of men like Löwe, Schalk and Nikisch, his symphonies established themselves, and more and more conductors rose to the challenge. At the same time he attracted increasing attention from writers – not on the biographical level but in articles and essays by prominent scholars who set out to explain, and provide critical analyses of, his works. A whole body of literature emerged with the aim of supplying the theoretical arguments with the help of which the case for Bruckner's music could be pleaded. August Halm,[3] for example, advanced the concept of two different musical cultures, the one being that of Bruckner (and also Bach), the other that of the 'Classics', like Mozart and Beethoven. A quiet, independently-minded musician who lived in Swabia, Halm had a considerable influence, especially through his ability to strike at the heart of the question under discussion. As Bruckner's music came under attack from those who took their stand on the 'Classics', so the rival camp launched a campaign in Bruckner's name against the Classics, and against Beethoven in particular. Halm and his followers even succeeded in convincing many people that, as far as the creation of musical form was concerned, Bruckner was not only Beethoven's equal, his heir, but in fact his superior.

The first thing to be said to this is that one cannot possibly apply Brucknerian criteria to Beethoven, any more than one can apply Beethovenian criteria to Bruckner. If one is going to have two different musical cultures, one must avoid comparing features of the one with features of the other. Propaganda of this kind does Bruckner no service. In fact, in a book on Beethoven which he wrote towards the end of his life, Halm substantially revised his earlier attitudes.

For all this, it cannot be denied that the Bruckner movement is well on the way to making up for what Bruckner himself never experienced, *viz.* the creation – the miscreation, rather – of a kind of orthodoxy. There are two aspects to movements of such a kind. There were once orthodox 'Wagnerians' and orthodox 'Brahmsians', rival groupings who may have served a purpose in their day but who in the long run have caused only confusion. Goethe used to complain about the Germans' tiresome habit of playing one person off against another. It would be better, he said, if, instead of racking their brains over who was the greater, he or Schiller, they would count themselves fortunate to have two such 'fellows' in their midst.

In practical terms, of course, the argument of Wagner versus Brahms has long since been resolved. We are well aware that music drama and absolute music can exist perfectly happily side by side. Yet Wagnerians and Brahmsians continue to survive, together with the old enmities. It even looks as though the argument of Brahms versus Bruckner, which is a kind of by-product of Brahms versus Wagner, will also refuse to die.

I do not want to be misunderstood on this. I have nothing against a body of enthusiastic supporters of a great man – I prefer that ten times to blasé, pseudo-historical attitudes that try to make all values relative. Art is akin to love, and in art, above all, the greater the love, the more profound the knowledge. Why, in art, love of the one should exclude love of the other, is something I fail to understand.

The familiar clichés one hears about Bruckner tell us little.

Some praise him as a champion of Catholicism, others as the embodiment of the Upper Austrian countryside where he was born. But these are peripheral truths – they cannot reach to the heart of the man. Even to apostrophize him as the incarnation of the Germanic spirit in music is of little help – one might say the same about Brahms. And one has reason to become suspicious when, on the basis of often highly tendentious anecdotes, he is presented as a naive, simpleminded character who never lost his childhood faith – a touching figure, in his way, but not to be taken all that seriously. It is not a rare phenomenon – a feeling of envy on the part of mediocre, small-minded people, unable to deny the stature of the great but desperate for some failings to pin on them. Wagner's 'bad character', Beethoven's 'pathological bitterness', Brahms' 'petty-mindedness', Bruckner's 'intellectual inferiority' – all these are symptoms of the same tendency.

The subject becomes particularly critical when those who profess so great an admiration for Bruckner's naturalness and religious faith turn out to be the very ones with the least idea of what is natural and what faith means – radicals and urban intellectuals who have made something of a cult of his music in recent years. Great works of art do not emerge without a maximum of intellectual effort and *engagement* on the part of their creator. There has never been an artist who, in a state of trance, produced works that transcended his general intellectual capacity. If Bruckner seems like a stranger in the real world, it is because he paid too little heed to it. In return he was so much more at his ease in the world of art.

This is where the many articles and books that have been appearing on Bruckner in recent times have often done him a disservice, presenting a false, distorted picture of the man and his work. The quiet grandeur of his noble personality is in danger of becoming a subject for fiction. Does he deserve such a fate?

Bruckner's admirers, like everyone else, must face the facts. And one fact is that his music has hitherto never enjoyed more than limited success. It would be a mistake to imagine that, at the time it first appeared, this lack of success could be put down entirely to Hanslick.[4] Critics do not wield that kind of power. And we must bear in mind that among those who rejected and failed to understand his music were some of the foremost musicians of the time – Bülow, Brahms (who was full of admiration for Wagner) and conductors such as Weingartner and Wüllner, among many others.

The situation is much the same today. The worldwide reputation of Brahms is scarcely less than that of Wagner but Bruckner is rarely appreciated outside the German-speaking world. I have conducted symphonies of his in America, England and Italy but everywhere I have met this lack of understanding. Nor do I expect any change in the foreseeable future. Listeners in Romance countries, in particular, complain about the formlessness of his works, while there are general objections to his excessive use of sequential repetition, his stereotyped endings and so on.

It would lead me too far afield if I were to go more fully into these objections and complaints, whether justified or unjustified. But one thing does need to be said – not only to the Germans but to musical people the world over. This is, that in the last analysis these are not the things that really matter. The importance of a work of art – contrary to what inveterate critics and Philistines think – does not lie in an absence of faults, in technical perfection, but in the power and grandeur of the message. The fact that a work is polished in execution and offers little scope for criticism may help it to acquire international recognition but it says nothing about its real quality.

Some twenty or more years ago a number of distinguished musicians from all over the world were asked to decide what was the most important work in the whole of music. They voted, not for the St Matthew Passion, or for Beethoven's Ninth Symphony, or for Wagner's *Die Meistersinger* – but for Bizet's *Carmen*. This was no coincidence. If one's primary criteria are those of elegance, of urbanity, of consummate form, then *Carmen* is indeed in a class of its own.

But there are other qualities to look for which we Germans, in particular, find more appropriate, more to the point. And after one has taken into account all the shortcomings, real and alleged, of Bruckner's music, one is still left with a triumphant achievement of such majesty as will outweigh all these shortcomings a thousand times. No-one who has genuinely experienced this music can fail to recognize its profundity, its purity, its sense of dedication. Its failings, moreover, seem somehow to be part and parcel of the achievement as a whole. Bruckner is one of the few geniuses in the whole history of music whose appointed task was to express the transcendental in human terms, to weave the power of God into the fabric of human life.

Be it in struggles against the forces of the underworld, or in music of blissful transfiguration, his whole mind and spirit were infused with thoughts of the divine, of God above and God on earth. He was, in fact, not a musician but a mystic, in the line of men like Meister Eckart and Jakob Böhme. Is it surprising that he walked the earth like a stranger, a man for whom the world in itself held no interest, had no meaning? And is it not immaterial whether such a man is a cobbler – as Böhme was – or a choirmaster from Upper Austria?

Artists like Bruckner are like erratic blocks, reminders of a former age, linked only loosely to their historical environment and explicable only to a limited degree in terms of that environment. Hence the lack of understanding that such artists face during their lifetime. But at the same time they command our attention, force us to confront them. One can either look them straight in the eye or pass by on the other side. A composer like Bruckner demands from his listeners total dedication, total surrender. This then, in its turn, yields its own priceless rewards.

But the outside world has little idea what it is like for an artist to have such a cross to bear. It behoves us at least to preserve a sense of gratitude and humility, and to be mindful of the fact that it is to divine providence that we, as a nation, owe the presence in our midst of such prophets, geniuses who hold up a mirror to mankind.

If we now pose the question, what light can a composer such as Bruckner cast on our own path through life, and what significance does he have for our future, it is as much a question about ourselves as about Bruckner. In terms of personality, as I have indicated, he was a strange mixture – peasant and child of the people on the one hand, sensitive musician, receptive to experiences of the most sublime exaltation on the other. Such a combination of rude earthiness and intense intellectuality is not all that rare among German composers. Haydn, Beethoven, Schubert, Brahms – these may be reckoned among his spiritual companions, though the extremes seem more pronounced in Bruckner. People often maintain that these are not just extremes but inner contradictions, incapable of existing side by side. But this is not so. Experience has shown that many creative geniuses, especially in music, have been able to accommodate the dichotomy, and the proclivity of Bruckner's genius to monumentality and simple grandeur, to a universality of meaning and message, is connected with this.

Heir to the innovations and techniques of the Romantic age, Bruckner lived at a time when the wholeness of the musical experience was being split up into a mass of separate stimuli. He accepted unquestioningly whatever techniques he found in use, making no attempt to ignore them, yet he remained true to himself. He alone among his contemporaries seemed to possess the power to put to his own use a musical world created by Wagner for quite different purposes – the power possessed by Siegfried, to wear the Nibelung's ring without being stricken by the curse which brings destruction down on the head of all others. This sets him above and beyond his time. He has a message of vital relevance for our own age, a message of universal validity which goes beyond the expression of individual genius and reaches, like that of Brahms and the great composers of the past, to the heart of human experience. This is the point at which Bruckner's destiny and ours coincide.

Let us be under no illusion. The urge to convey a message of 'universal validity', as I called it, has become progressively weaker in recent times. The appeals one hears from all quarters to make music universally accessible, to produce 'art for the people' and so on, are something quite different. Indeed, they only go to show the extent to which modern composers have lost touch with the needs and interests of the people. One must draw a strict distinction between an object that has the validity of universal experience and one that is simply universally accessible. It is like the difference between a melody by Beethoven and a pop song. Accessibility, i.e. the quality of being comprehensible on the most banal of levels, frequently goes hand in hand with extreme individualism. But even the artist who is shamelessly preoccupied with his own ego is in some way a member of the community: it is just that this community no longer represents the goal to which he aspires, is no longer his source of inspiration and encouragement, no longer provides the context of his creativity. He abandons it to mere conventions, mere banalities: what matters to him is not union with the community as such but the sign under which the union takes place. The expression of universal experience, on the other hand, is directed towards a genuine spiritual communion. And this is the true mark of greatness.

Let us look at the matter historically. The universal validity of artistic expression was far greater in earlier, unsophisticated periods than it became later. As time went on and the consciousness of theoretical issues and artistic techniques grew, this val-

idity becomes increasingly hard to find, until we reach the paradoxical state of affairs where it is no longer the man from the
midst of the masses, the proverbial 'simple soul' mirroring the
popular taste of the day, that gives expression to these universal
truths in his nobility and his simplicity, but the individual
genius, alone in his greatness. In ages like ours, which have
lost their innocence, it is only given to the man of great strength
to find his way through the jungle of traditional values and
acquired interests. Complexity has become the convention of
our time. It is only the greatest minds that refuse to be caught
up in this convention and plough their lonely furrow towards
the goal of simplicity – a very special simplicity, by means of
which they restore to mankind its lost spiritual unity. As a
result the eighteenth-century concept of the artistic genius has
begun to acquire a special significance for the present day. He
has become a necessity. He enables us to rediscover ourselves.

It is important that we understand this, the more so since the
concept of genius tends to be regarded with great suspicion.
There are good reasons for this. There is a natural resentment
of a situation in which the many are at the mercy of the whims
of the few. But it is not the people, the public, who think this
way – they have always been natural worshippers of genius,
followers of the cult of genius. The suspicion comes from artists,
especially mediocre artists. And if the combined efforts of critics,
historians and artists have not succeeded in toppling the genius
from his throne, then it is in essence only a sign – and there
are but few – of how profoundly we still need art, true art,
today.

It would be interesting to investigate why and how it should
be in the age of late Rococo that this concept of genius emerged.
Related to it, likewise a product of the Age of Goethe and a
powerful force throughout the nineteenth century, is the concept of the 'Classic' – an ideal of order and perfection, resting
on value judgements which identify the Good and the True and
thereby testify involuntarily, to the values of the age itself. But
this ideal too appears utterly discredited today.

These two concepts, the Genius and the 'Classic', are not only
related to each other but also have a common origin in what I
called the 'universal validity' of artistic expression. All three are
out of tune with the times, and for the same reasons. A large
share of the responsibility for this development lies with the
relativistic, so-called 'historical' approach which made its
appearance in the Romantic era. The 'Classic', which, in the

sense in which I use it here, has nothing to do with Antiquity and embraces Beethoven and Kleist equally with Goethe and Schiller, is committed to the Absolute and is deliberately anti-historical. But it is precisely the desire and intention to understand and interpret works of art in terms of their historical context that distinguishes our age from earlier ages, including the nineteenth century. One might go so far as to claim that a capacity for historical thinking is the greatest intellectual achievement of the modern era. But it has proven to be a mixed blessing.

Those of us who believe in the absoluteness and the innocence of life have often pointed out that by viewing things as historically conditioned, we destroy our own previously unconditional relationship to the universe. By seeing contemporary events primarily in relation to their environment, we relegate their relationship to ourselves to an issue of secondary importance and thereby deprive ourselves of the opportunity to respond directly to these events. Instead of being active, thinking arbiters, we suddenly become mere onlookers, spectators – spectators who can cast their gaze over an infinitely wider area but at the cost of a loss of involvement, an impoverishment of life itself.

When a new work of art appears, it has first to be catalogued, filed in its appropriate place. Large, small, progressive, old-fashioned – we need to know where it belongs. The question of the significance of a particular man or a particular work in the context of history is considered more important than that of its significance for us as contemporary men and women. Is not an attitude of this kind calculated, in the last analysis, to relieve us of the need to make up our own minds, form our own judgements? Indeed, does it not so permeate our thoughts and emotions that – perverse as the conclusion may seem – we no longer dare to be natural and begin to harbour serious doubts about the value of our own existence?

This is a state of affairs that has not been found at any other time in history. What it means is that modern man has nothing firm to hold on to, nothing that claims his mind and his allegiance, nothing in which he can see his own existence and his own nature reflected. Art no longer speaks to him in the language of his own being or his own destiny. This means that art has made itself superfluous. It is at an end. It has become a vehicle of education, a source of indulgence – an education which is an indulgence because we could easily dispense with it.

The whole process is already so far advanced that one is bound to be caught up in the theory of the situation. Never have we heard so much theorizing about the function of art in society and the like. But there is no agreement over how such an art is to be brought about. This, however, is precisely where the nub of the problem lies.

To pursue the matter further here would lead us too far afield. For the moment we have not got beyond the grey area of theory and speculation.[5] Musicians – both composers and performers – are discreetly and somewhat shamefacedly trying to retrace their steps towards the paths that they had begun to follow thirty years earlier, as though they cannot make up their minds what practical conclusions to draw, if any, from what critics and theorists are telling us. The same applies to the public who continue, in spite of being surrounded by ceaseless chatter about Neo-Objectivity, communal art and the rest, to pay homage to unrestrained individualism and pursue an unaffected cult of personality.

One thing I must add. The urge to acquire an objective, supra-personal style does not guarantee an art of universal validity. Such an intention may be formed in the mind but it leaves the vital sphere, the actual creative source of art, untouched. An art of universal validity involves the whole man. An inevitable consequence of an exclusively intellectual approach is that the vital creative sphere sacrifices its role as the source of true art and degenerates into banality. This has in turn given rise to the irreconcilable conflict that has only today become so apparent between serious music and light music, the former expressive of a life weighed down with problems of one kind or another, the latter reflecting a desire for unconsidered and trivial enjoyment.

Universal validity of experience can only be achieved when 'Above' and 'Below' have ceased to be irreconcilable opposites, when the nobility of divine nature manifests itself in the humble world of the common people, and when in his supreme moments of sublime inspiration the artist never loses the consciousness of standing with his feet firmly planted in his beloved Mother Earth.

Which returns us to Bruckner, for such an artist was he. This is why he claims our affection. There is not a single note in his music, through the whole gamut of human emotions, that does not link us, and him, in some way to the world of the eternal. He has shown that even in the modern world the challenge to universal validity of expression can still be laid down, and that to strive for simplicity, purity, grandeur and power of expression can still be a feature of art and life today.

11 Hindemith

A campaign has been launched in certain circles against Paul Hindemith on the grounds that he is 'not acceptable' to the new Germany. Why? What is he accused of?

In the first place, of 'political' offences. He is said to be of Jewish descent and to have played viola for years in the Amar Quartet, which he founded and some of whose members are Jewish.[1] It is also claimed that since the National-Socialist revolution he has made gramophone records in company with two Jewish musicians who have since emigrated. This refers to a string trio which had been in existence for years before the revolution. Nor were the other two members 'emigrés'. One was Szymon Goldberg,[2] an outstanding violinist, leader of the Berlin Philharmonic Orchestra, who left the orchestra only a few months ago in order to pursue a career as soloist. The other was Emanuel Feuermann,[3] an Austrian who had been for many years a highly-respected teacher at the Staatliche Hochschule für Musik in Berlin and is generally recognized to be one of the best cellists in Europe. Moreover, the recordings in question were the final items in a long-standing contract.

Hindemith's opponents themselves are well aware that these are not the real reasons for the attacks on him. The principal source lies in those of his works which are open to criticism from an ideological point of view, in particular on the grounds of certain of the texts he has chosen to set to music.

It must be conceded that the libretti of the three one-act operas *Mörder, Hoffnung der Frauen, Nusch-Nuschi* and *Sancta Susanna* are extremely dubious.[4] The same applies to the *Badener Lehrstück* and to *Neues vom Tage* – which is little more than a revue. However, we must remember that the three one-acters are juvenilia. At the time he wrote them, Hindemith was by no means sure whether he wanted to be a composer. And without drawing comparisons of any other kind, one may well ask whether their subject-matter is in any way more perverse than that, say, of the mature Richard Strauss' *Salome*. And who is prepared to turn his back on Strauss because of the libretto of *Salome*? The prime responsibility for the choice of such subjects – in the case of both Strauss and Hindemith – lies with the age in which each was written, which had a penchant for such scandalous material, and Hindemith's efforts to keep as close as possible to the taste of the age is thoroughly understandable in an era when questions were being increasingly raised about the relationship between the artist and the public. Hindemith knew, as did Strauss, that Wagner could not have written his operas of love and redemption without sharing the spiritual assumptions of his age. Hindemith was too honest to try and follow in Wagner's footsteps. If one wishes to see what kind of libretto corresponds to Hindemith's real nature, one must turn to that which he wrote – the only time he has been his own librettist – for his latest opera, only recently completed, called *Mathis der Maler*.[5] No-one who reads it can fail to detect, among many other qualities, its profound sense of moral commitment. Some maintain that he has just changed tack in response to the changed circumstances. Quite apart from the fact that he would be totally incapable of reacting in such a way, the accusation is totally without foundation, since the work was begun long before the National-Socialist revolution.

So much for the question of Hindemith's texts. As to the music, that of the three one-act operas testifies to a considerable talent and contain passages of great vitality. Like a large proportion of his purely instrumental music of the time, such as the Organ Concerto, the slightly later opera *Neues vom Tage* shows the technical mastery that never deserted him but also a good deal of mechanical, rather empty passage-work, which caused him to be widely identified in Germany with the then fashionable anti-Romantic cult of 'Neo-Objectivity'[6] or 'Neo-Classicism', inaugurated by Stravinsky. Today, in an age with a quite different outlook, it is easy to reject this cult and make Hindemith the scapegoat for the excesses of his theoretical partners. But it would be wrong to do so, the more so since most of his works from this period were hastily written occasional pieces, with the emphasis of his activity shifting increasingly from 'pure' composition to works for practical use – so-called *Gebrauchsmusik*.

Still active as a soloist,[7] Hindemith now began to devote more time to teaching. This was an activity for which, with his insistance on a high degree of technical ability – here he puts us in mind of the old masters – he seemed predestined, especially through his rare ability to understand young people and sense their needs. A whole generation of school and college students owe their musical education to him, and no other composer has such a following among the young. He devoted particular attention to school music, tirelessly seeking ways of bridging the deplorable gulf that has opened up between folk-music and art-music. His work in this field coincides with trends characteristic of our new National-Socialist Germany – his *Plöner Musiktag*, for instance, was a pioneering work in the field of school music.

In the broader context Hindemith first attracted attention with his String Quartet Opus 16,[8] a work which, together with others that soon followed, stimulated a whole generation of chamber-music composers. True, not many of the works of these composers amounted to more than experiments but Hindemith can scarcely be blamed for that. His own works from this early period are notable for their blend of structural mastery, emotional reserve and a special feeling for the demands of chamber music on the one hand, and a fresh, carefree vitality, even daring, coupled with a direct, introspective lyricism – particularly in the slow movements – on the other.

His reputation also spread abroad, not merely on account of his skill as a performer but increasingly by virtue of the progressive, pioneering qualities in his works. He deliberately broke with the emotionalism of the Wilhelminian era, the false Romanticism that still lingered in the wake of Wagner and Richard Strauss, and instead of making his music serve philosophical ideas or wallowing in an indulgent Neo-Romantic sentimentality, like many of his contemporaries, he cultivated the values of straightforwardness, objectivity and simplicity.

On the strength of these early works – to which one could add a number from later periods, such as the song-cycle *Das Marienleben*[9] – one arrives at an image of Hindemith (who has pure Germanic blood in his veins) as an out-and-out German type – German in his direct and honest craftsmanship and his open, rugged nature as well as in the purity and restraint of his comparatively rare displays of emotion.

His most recent work, the symphony from *Mathis der Maler*, has served to confirm these qualities. Since its first performance in March 1934 it has made a deep impression wherever it has been played, notably on those not otherwise particularly well-disposed towards him. This does not signify, I repeat, any ideological change of direction on his part but rather a return to his beginnings, to his real self.

Eight months ago, when the *Mathis* Symphony was first heard, the authorities made no move against Hindemith, perhaps because of an unconscious reluctance to interfere in the course of the nation's culture. Now, although he has published nothing in the meantime, they have decided to mount a campaign of public vilification against him with the object of forcing him to leave the country. No tactic seems too petty. They have even sunk to the depths of quoting the occasional parody of Wagner and Puccini in his works, completely missing the point of such badinage.[10] Obviously, with a composer who has written so much and whose works are there in published form for everybody to inspect, it is not difficult, years after the event, to find youthful indiscretions. Moreover Hindemith has never engaged in political activity. Where will it lead if we begin to apply the methods of political denunciation to art?

There can be no doubt but that no musician of his generation has done more for the reputation of German music throughout the world than Paul Hindemith. How the future will judge his compositions is, of course, something we cannot tell today. In any case this is not the point at issue. What concerns us here is a matter of general principle which takes us far beyond the particular case of Hindemith. But let there be no misunderstanding. Given the incredible paucity of really creative composers in the world today, we cannot afford to turn our backs like this on a man of the calibre of Hindemith.

Part III
On Art and Life

12 Thoughts for All Seasons

The pages that follow reflect the point of view of a musician, a representative of the arts. It is not normally the business of an artist to make general observations in philosophical terms, and I am well aware that to try and compress my thoughts into so limited a space will only make for dissatisfaction in many quarters. Indeed, I would have given a great deal to be spared this effort. The reason I cannot avoid doing so lies with the contemporary situation, which unhappily demands from all artists a degree of awareness and certainty about the nature of art which was not necessary in earlier and happier times. Given the incredible ideological confusion that prevails today, an awareness of the situation can offer the artist a measure of reassurance and help him preserve his integrity in the face of an over-intellectualized environment.

Let us consider the activity of artistic creation. One might fairly describe it as a struggle. The conflicts that provoke this struggle have their roots in the substance, the material (in the broadest sense) of the art in question – its forms, colours, harmonies and so on. The artist's task is to harness the forces inherent in this substance to a single common purpose. Before he sets to work on it, it is in a wild, natural, unordered state. This is more immediately obvious in architecture and music than in the visual arts and poetry, although it is equally applicable here. As the composer regards the elements of his raw material in his hand, he sees an endless series of possibilities in his struggle to unite the various stresses and tensions in that material, with its underlying laws of rhythm, harmony and so on, and produce his final integrated product.

When we look more closely at this process, we find we can distinguish two levels. On the first each individual element combines with those adjacent to it to form larger elements, these larger elements then combining with others and so on, a logical outwards growth from the part to the whole. On the other level the situation is the reverse: the given unity of the whole controls the behaviour of the individual elements within it, down to the smallest detail. The essential thing to observe is that in any genuine work of art these two levels complement each other, so that the one only becomes effective when put together with the other. Not until today, when the essential unity of the two levels has dissolved, have we been in a position to perceive the distinction between them.

These two levels or aspects of the creative process only make up what we might call the skeleton of the work of art. But philosophical investigation of the matter will take us no further. The next step would be to adduce the analogy of the personality of the creative artist. For to correspond to the two kinds of creative process there are two kinds of subjective personality. Corresponding to the power that works inwards, from the whole to the parts, a power which proceeds from a more or less complete vision of the whole, is an emotion that springs from the artist's relationship to the world at its most profound and most meaningful, an emotion one may call love, humility, reverence, worship, awe and many other things.

The other kind of creative process, however, although broadly directed by an overall view from above, is characterized by the gradual revelation of the whole in the course of its progress – a logical outwards growth from the part to the whole, as I put it above – corresponding to an urge to understand and control the world in its physical manifestations. It is this urge that inspires the artist at the inception of his work and drives him onward from one moment to the next, starting with the smallest element and working upwards, each element larger than the last. But such an artist is yet guided by a vision of the whole which resides in the recesses of his unconscious mind. For the two are inseparable – a passionate desire to understand the world in its every living detail, and a love of that same world, which comes to us as the eternal gift of God. If only modern man would grasp that it is impossible to understand and shape the world as it confronts us without loving it! And that it is equally impossible to love it without seeking, in the context of this love, to understand it!

The artistic process that has as its starting-point the unity of the whole rests on the concept of a more-or-less complete vision of that whole. For the artist at work – work being, in this context, not a state, a condition but a dynamic activity of struggle and victory – this vision is the goal he seeks to attain, the star that, unbeknown to him, guides his steps through the maze of obstacles and temptations that beset his path and shows him how to unite the forces at his command. Only at the end of the journey, therefore, will the vision emerge in its totality, not only for the listener, the receiver of the work of art, but also – and this is a vital point – for the composer, the creative artist himself. The total vision only achieves its full radiance when it merges with all the individual sources of light from within the work, the overall and the particular interacting and stimulating each other. It is not that the vision is present, ready-made, from the beginning and is only waiting to be filled with artistic substance. On the contrary: the joy that the artist feels comes not from possessing the vision but from the activity of turning it into reality. (The question of the nature of the vision before it receives aesthetic form, and in particular of the way in which the forces that issue from the vision combine with those which are present in the artistic material, is a subject in itself.)

Thus the vision really only appears in its fullness through its embodiment in the work of art, and the question often raised today about the extent of an artist's vision, how grand, or otherwise, his conception, without consideration of whether his material contains the forces necessary to give expression to that vision, is pointless. And if one uses it as the basis for a value judgement, it becomes positively misleading. I repeat: it is not the greatness of the vision that counts but the realization of that vision, the artistic form in which it is embodied, with the vision itself then, but only then, included as part of that embodiment.

The extent to which this situation is no longer understood, with the separation of vision and artistic material taken for granted and widely accepted as a natural concomitant of the development of art, is apparent from the common use of terms such as 'idealism' and 'realism', terms which collapse in the face of any true work of art. It is thus only of secondary import- ance to which of these two types an artist belongs. The com- poser, by virtue of his material, belongs by nature to the 'ideal- ist' camp. As he has lost the strength to realize his vision, so also has he lost his feeling for the necessity of this realization. The consequence is that either he provides his works with a vision in the shape of a literary text, an idea or a programme and tries to convey to his listeners in conceptual form what he is unable to convey in emotional terms, or he abandons this approach as well and loses all direct contact with his public. The vision continues to exist only for his own benefit, and the music becomes clouded, imprecise. It stutters instead of speaking. As the naturalist observes instead of shaping his work, so the idealist – in our case the composer – feels instead of shaping his work. But are we obliged to listen to a language that we only half comprehend – indeed, which is only semi-comprehensible?

The nature of the composer's raw material plays a part in this. This material is not amenable to naturalistic treatment like that of the painter or sculptor. As a result a number of dangers and possible errors disappear as far as the composer is concerned. Virtually anything in music that one can call 'naturalistic' is conveyed by rhythm, in that rhythm can reflect the course of an actual event. But since the rhythmic element is only part of the whole reality of such an event, that event cannot itself be portrayed in music but only imagined, or guessed at, by the listener through association. Musical naturalism of this kind tends to find its natural place in the theatre, receiving its meaning from the actions and events that take place on the stage. Alternatively, as in programme music, the listener has to project the event or events on to the music (apart from the fact that this is possible in only the broadest of terms, it cannot but be a somewhat crude operation and something of an imposition on the listener, whose good will it considerably taxes).

But if rhythm makes a certain kind of naturalism possible, harmony totally excludes it. (The portrayal of bleating sheep, or of a child screaming in the bath, is not done by harmonic effects but by reproducing the actual pitch of the sounds on particular instruments of the orchestra.) The sound of a single concrete harmony transports us at once into the realm of art, far from the world of objective reality.

It is not part of my purpose to embark on a discussion of the principles underlying the art of music – in view of the state of music today and of the total confusion in aesthetic matters, it would take volumes to cover the subject. This much, however, I will say: the existence of music as an art is linked to the capacity to experience a sound, any sound, as something self-contained, something with a life of its own, a piece of living reality. Only from such a starting-point is it possible to conceive the existence of objective aesthetic form. The musical forms that have developed in the course of history are only the rich and diverse manifestations of a law whose basic expression is the cadence. The works of the great masters, the fugues of Bach, the symphonies of Beethoven, are all subject to this formal law, a law laid upon them by nature. Furthermore the original musical achievements accomplished in the time between Chopin and Wagner on the one hand and Pfitzner, Debussy and Richard Strauss on the other, all spring from the same source, even if often only in part and with a different kind of relationship to the whole.

All genuine development, right down to the present day, derives on the one hand from the expansion and enrichment of the relationships arising from these basic conditions, and on the other from a growing concentration and intensification of the innate forces within them. These forces are taken for granted, and their existence would only be questioned if we were to decide to express ourselves in a different tonal system – a system of quarter-tones, for example. Such a system could not, however, develop from our present system, any more than an apple-tree could be grafted on to an oak.

Behind all these speculations on the possibility of things such as a quarter-tone system[1] lies the idea, conscious or unconscious, of progress, an idea which tyrannizes our thoughts – thus also our art – in a way no Inquisition, no religious superstition ever did in the past. How has this come about?

The artist's embodiment of his vision in the work of art is identical with his awareness of the vision itself. The inner forces of his material hold the vision together, and the more tightly they do so, the more conscious he becomes of the reality of the vision. This consciousness is coterminous with the creative process and arises at the moment when the artist taps in his material the force that will express the vision to the full. Consciousness informs him when the creative process has run its course: his activity ceases, and with it his joy in the work in question, which is now finished. Consciousness thus holds within itself the terms of the relationship between the artistic material and the vision this material is to embody – that is to say, the artist ultimately discovers through his own labours how to give expression to this feature and that. Once acquired, this is knowledge he can never lose; it will remain with him through all his future works. Consciousness is thus the equivalent of reaching, more or less involuntarily, the end of the creative process. Once one has reached one's goal, it is impossible to reach it again, and senseless to contemplate the possibility. The senselessness of setting out to repeat a successful work, to state a second time what has been already satisfactorily stated once, confirms the law of nature whereby we employ all the powers at our disposal only when confronted with something new, something unfamiliar, i.e. something that has not yet forced its way into our consciousness.

Once an artist has learnt how to express a particular thing, he will employ this knowledge again in the future, like the application of a known fact to a new situation. What originally had its own purpose now becomes a link in a new chain; it becomes a means to an end and loses its independent status. This is the way in which all progress, all development takes place, both in the general and in the particular. This, of course, refers specifically to the individual units of expression within the body of the work of art and not to the work as a whole, which is an end, a goal in itself, and cannot be treated as a part of something new. The artist's consciousness of the whole presents him with both the necessity and the opportunity to create something completely new, a completely new world which has nothing to do with old worlds. Hence the fact that the greatest artists, those who have given the fullest and grandest expression to their visions, are also those who have created the most varied works. The greatest artists were the most versatile and most universal. They were also the most deeply committed, but this commitment was never directed to what lay in front of them but to what lay behind them, not to their activity as such but to the skill and knowledge they brought to bear on that activity. Instead of 'the most deeply committed' one might call them 'those possessed of the greatest knowledge'.

All this is a matter for the individual artist. The more capable he is of giving full creative form to his subject-matter, the more complete and fulfilled will be the life enjoyed by his works, the more self-sufficient and independent of their creator. He, in turn, will have greater freedom to shape each succeeding work from a completely new point of departure: nothing will be left over from the preceding work, in which everything, so to speak, has been used up.

As far as the individual elements drawn from the material of his art are concerned, they also undergo a development at the hands of the individual artist but only to a limited extent. Even those whose art was subject to a great many changes in the course of their career retain a basic consistency in their approach to their material in respect of technique, however much the subject-matter of one work may differ from that of another. The artist's signature is everywhere recognizable.

This consistency is what first strikes the layman's attention and gives rise to epithets such as Shakespearian, Wagnerian and so on. Contrary to the opinion widely held in cultural circles, such terms convey no significant information. Rather, the individuality of the artist in question reveals itself only in the particular work itself: the way he approaches his material is only a conditioning factor, the means by which he arrives at the creation of his work, of his world. It does, however, share with this world the fact that the artist, as an individual human being, is inseparably bound to that world.

The situation becomes different if we consider these individual elements not in terms of their kinship to each other, the ways in which they come together to form groups in the hands of this artist or that, but as independent products of the artist's material. They are of necessity irreducible units, i.e. they cannot but remain isolated elements vis-à-vis the whole because they embody a direct and absolute relationship to the material and can therefore be separated from the personality of the individual artist. These are the elements which make possible the development of art independently of, and, as it were, over the head of, the individual artist. In contrast to his basic approach to his material, the means by which the artist creates his own world, and in even greater contrast to this world itself, which appears in unique form in each successive work, these individual elements undergo a process of development in which the earlier elements are subsumed, cancelled out, by the subsequent elements. Thus a modern composer cannot take over the harmonic range of Wagner, say, or Schumann, let alone Mozart, because the harmonic material itself has developed – irresistibly, automatically, from inner impulsion. It is a development no-one can resist or escape, and constitutes what one calls the 'style' of a particular epoch. As such it is common to the most insignificant achievements of that epoch as to its greatest, and has hardly anything to do with art itself – even less than has what I described above as the individual artist's basic approach to his material. It lends itself rather to explanation in theoretical terms.

Since these units of expression are only parts of a whole, they can in practice only be employed in the context of a whole; and however much their selection and character depend on the content of the whole, on them in turn depends the character of that whole. Since this material is subject to its own internally-generated development, without reference to the whole, but at the same time there exists the closest of interrelationships between it and this whole, the forces that govern the whole must coincide with the state of development reached by the material, if both are to achieve their expressive purpose. This explains why a particular art emerges at a particular time: it is because the aims of the age as a whole coincide with the potentialities latent in the material. It also explains phenomena which history alone cannot explain, for example, how Baroque flourished in art and architecture at a time when Bach and his predecessors were composing a music governed rather by the formal principles of Gothic. It is a mistake to try and explain an historical phenomenon exclusively in terms of either one side of the equation or the other – the development of the material in its own right or the creative tendency of the age. But if one were forced to choose, priority would have to be given to the latter. It is highly probable that the reason why the creative spirit of a particular age could not express itself in this art form or that, is that the state of the development of the material in that art did not match that creative spirit.

The developmental forces present in the material cannot but make themselves felt also in the work as a whole. Historical development shows this very clearly. To start with, artists had to familiarize themselves with the possibilities latent in the material of their art. They started on the simplest of levels, knowing, however, that purely on the basis of the forces within the material the wholeness of the work was guaranteed. This sense of wholeness provided the unconscious foundation of their creativity but it could not in itself be the object of that creativity because the separate elements were at that stage still ends in themselves and demanded the artist's entire attention.

As a result, the whole, although an organic compound of separate elements, had not yet achieved real independence. In Haydn and Mozart, for example, the various forms taken by the whole, such as the sonata and the symphony, are, comparatively speaking, the most conventional, least fully defined aspect of their music. The form was in essence already there, an organic synthesis of elements; it was in these elements themselves that the real vitality of the work lay. Later, especially with Beethoven, the situation changed, and the elements, now individually absorbed and mastered, and accepted into the aesthetic consciousness of the age, combined to form ever larger units. As the logical sequence of the parts grew, so did the cohesiveness of the whole. The parts increasingly lost their independence, to the point where they were incomprehensible without reference to the whole; no part made sense without reference to that which preceded it and that which followed.

Examples of this can be found in Beethoven's late works, with their increasing acceptance of the consequences resulting from this development process.

Up to the time of Beethoven musical development had taken place within the tacit assumption that the work of art emerged like an organism. Those forces in the material which corresponded to this conception were called upon and exploited. But now these forces too became victims of the process of conscious development. Whereas Beethoven, following both his basic attitude to his material and the nature of his genius, sought to bring out the whole with ever greater clarity and power, his contemporaries such as Weber, but even more his successors in the Romantic movement, turned away from this approach. The concept of the work of art as an organic whole crumbled in their hands. The Romantics remained faithful to it only in small forms, and it was not long before the grand ideals of the past were forgotten altogether.

Then came Wagner, with a new view of the whole, creating a new unity in the form of drama and adding a whole series of new material elements. The nature of the whole as seen by Wagner gave rise to a more intense exploitation of the material, an intensity encouraged by the fact that this exploitation was less concerned with the logical sequence of the elements in a purely musical sense. But as a result the material as such was all the more quickly exhausted, and Wagner's successors, who lack the Master's own very personal sense of unity sustained by drama, now face total bankruptcy. They are not interested in a unity created by following the laws of the musical material itself, like that sought by Brahms in taking his lead from the great masters of the past, while the unity offered by Wagner is not open to them, since they work only as composers, not as creators of a *Gesamtkunstwerk*. Viewed in this light, the path that leads to programme music – in its naturalistic form in opera, in its conceptual form in the music of the concert hall – seems the only one remaining, if the necessity for any kind of form is not to be totally negated.

A similar situation obtains where the elements of musical language itself are concerned. We have reached a point where composers no longer dare to use simple, direct harmony for fear of repeating what has already been said. We are facing an impasse. One sign of this is the increasingly desperate search for absolute novelty, anything that is totally independent of the meanings derived from the old material. The theory of the quarter-tone system is a case in point.

Since the concept of overall form as the expression of the artist's vision has also been affected by the irresistible onward march of developments in the musical material itself, today that concept has lost its central, dominant position. No longer does it appear to be able to assert itself over the material. No longer is it the whole that controls the behaviour of the parts. No longer does the vision go hand in hand with the forces contained in the material; rather, it is the latter that has come to dominate the vision, determining the form of the whole and thus the vision itself. The whole has been consumed by the parts, with the result that not only is there no longer a whole but there are also no longer any parts, because these can only exist so long as there is a whole to which they can refer. Everything exhausts itself in the individual moment, no heed being paid either to what has gone before or to what follows. The consequence is a concentration on the effectiveness of the moment, effectiveness for its own sake, in harmony, in rhythm, in orchestration, and through numerous little titillating details.

All this may appear to justify the notion of progress. But it would be wrong to see the history of the arts only in terms of the development of their material and of the overall form linked to it. For this overall form itself is the expression of the artist's vision, and although the vision can only become reality through its interaction with the material – indeed, may well owe its existence in part to the stimulus of the material – it cannot possibly be derived from the material. The vision is the most direct, most immediate expression of the artist's relationship to the world. As such it lives its own life in the artist's mind, without thought of realization in formal terms, although, as we have seen, it only achieves its realization through the act of formal creation. It is not that the material seeks the appropriate vision on its own account but that the vision seeks the material for its complete expression. And since, as the expression of the artist's view of the world, the vision is something final, something ultimate, it is not capable of development in the manner of the material. The visions of two different artists are entirely separate from each other. One artist may influence another, and certain resemblances may become evident, but such resemblances can only be superficial, for every vision is by nature new, peculiar to the artist whose view of the world it embodies. Thus as history develops, the various visions, in their various embodiments, can come quite naturally to exist side by side. Unlike the situation with the material, no one vision is rendered invalid by the supervention of another. The great artists thus survive from one age to another, irrespective of the state of development of the material which they inherited and with which they worked. Phidias stands alongside Michelangelo, Bach alongside Beethoven, Mozart alongside Wagner.

Although there is no need of historical learning or any other intermediate agent for us to understand these facts, the majority of artists today refuse to face them. To the extent that they are guided by the feeling that the present state of their material, quite independently of the creative urges of the individual artist, requires a different kind of art from that of earlier ages, they are right to do so.

But they go much further than this. They deny categorically that the material is dependent on, and conditioned by, the vision, or that the parts are dependent on the whole. In fact, they deny that there is a whole. This leaves them with only the parts, i.e. the material in its present state of development, which, as we have seen, is subject to the law of progress and will eventually become exhausted. It is a process of complete materialization, the debasement of all the artistic elements present in the material, both cause and effect of the idea of progress. The significant features of a work of art, including the great works of the past, are now identified as lying only in the techniques employed – the harmony, the formal structure and so on – techniques, of course, corresponding to those which modern composers themselves admire and use. They cannot grasp what history would teach them – that every complex of material forces is in the last analysis only a means towards the realization of a vision, the creation of a living world, which is the sole purpose of all artistic activity. But when will we learn how to learn without imitating!

From the foregoing we can see that philosophical speculation has played a far larger part in the evolution of music in recent times than ever before. It is the source of the concept of progress we hear so much about today. And it is to a large extent people who have never experienced what it is to create a work of art, and where one derives the strength to do so, who decide how art is to 'develop'. They are prone to assess a work by its novelty – the novelty of its skills and techniques, that is to say. Even genuine composers cannot always escape from the influence of these people. The obsession with progress, with being original at all costs, hangs like the sword of Damocles over the heads of many modern composers, depriving them of the peace of mind they need in order to hear their own inner voice, and turning art from a free and joyful activity into soulless, pretentious drudgery.

For music, until recent times the most vital and vibrant of all the arts, to become caught up in this maelstrom of mechanical progress, a special constellation of circumstances was required. These circumstances are primarily the result of the activities of one man – Wagner. But the enormous influence that Wagner has had on modern music – and nowhere else in the history of art has a single individual ever exerted such an influence – is largely the result of a misconception. Wagner himself sensed the possibility of this misconception and it was this that turned him into a writer. If one were to summarize in two sentences the basic, ever-recurrent content of his writings, they would be 1), I am a poet, not a composer, and 2), the language which expresses the profoundest truths of the human soul is music. Put another way, this paradox, real or apparent, means: the total vision of my work is of a different nature, i.e. poetic, from that of the means, i.e. musical, through which it is to be realized.

Anybody with a knowledge of aesthetics must find this grotesque. Indeed, in the whole history of aesthetics from Aristotle down to the present day there would not be a single moment when one would have given any art which made such claims the slightest chance of survival. The fact that Wagner established himself in spite of this leads us to considerations in which lies the key to understanding the most deep-seated problems of our age. These considerations are not our concern at this moment. We need, however, to give our minds to the question of the effects that this aesthetic has had on music itself.

One thing that immediately strikes our attention when we look at Wagner's music is its complete lack of traditional forms – *Liedform*, sonata and so on. Viewed as a piece of music, a work by Wagner is sheer chaos, with no beginning, middle or end but simply an accumulation of small, self-contained sections. Where such formal elements are found, as in his early works, in *Parsifal* and, as part of the historical content, in *Die Meistersinger*, they do not emerge naturally from the heart of the work but are treated either in an arbitrary, fragmented manner or agglomerated in the style we associate with Baroque. Yet in spite of this the effect left by an opera of Wagner's is

not one of chaos but one of absolute precision and singlemindedness.

If we stand back and view the whole *qua* whole, allowing it
to make its natural effect on us, we begin to take the music for
what it is, namely, as a means of bringing the overall poetic
conception of the work to life. A number of things then become
clear which, like the technique of the Leitmotif, first seemed like
anti-artistic, rationalistic devices. It becomes clear that Wagner's
purpose is not to create a self-contained, self-sufficient music
which first absorbs the generative moments in the action, then
returns them to the world, new-born, so to speak, as in the
traditional opera; his purpose is simply to use the music to fill
the poetic text with life, with blood. It is a music conceived and
composed by a poet, not by a musician.

Thus Wagner's creativity manifests itself not, as with 'pure'
composers, in inventing and exploiting new forms but in discovering new musical styles. Each successive work is couched
in its own independent and individual style, distinct from that
of all other works, and that style infiltrates the smallest detail
of that work, so that in the case of two works written one
immediately after the other, like *Tristan und Isolde* and *Die Meistersinger*, it would be impossible to transfer a single bar from
one to the other without it becoming immediately obvious. The
overall vision, though only brought to life in the corresponding
musical style – Tristan's yearning for death, the bright, histori-
cally-coloured serenity of the Mastersingers – is perceived and
experienced first in poetic terms.

Simply to describe this situation – like everything else connected with Wagner's *Gesamtkunstwerk* – is easy. But to understand
it correctly is difficult. We are faced with the marriage of two
arts, a marriage unique in history, with immense consequences
for music, which have given rise to the innumerable misconceptions to which Wagner has been exposed, both during his lifetime and ever since. Misconceptions on the part of 'absolute'
musicians can easily be dispelled: they are genuine misconceptions, and those who reject Wagner on 'absolute' musical
grounds are by no means the worst of musicians. But there
are not many such musicians left. Far more dangerous are the
numerous misconceptions that derive from the way Wagner is
understood and interpreted today.

When musicians began to regard Wagner's music as absolute
music, as music *tout court*, it was inevitable that a revolution in
their attitudes would follow. What had formerly been rejected

now began to be seen as a new form of freedom, a release from the laws of thematic and harmonic composition, from the strict observance of the rules of organically developed form and from other constraints that had been felt to be so burdensome. To be sure, this led to the creation of a mass of new material elements in the post-Wagnerian period – opportunities for freer, more flexible forms, with more bold experiments in the last few years than in all the previous centuries of musical history put together. But very few of these 'experiments' proved to have any lasting or positive effect.

The most important aspect of the situation was that people's understanding of the meaning of music now took a new turn. They no longer felt the necessity for an organic musical whole, and the destruction of this concept opened the way to the developments that we see in modern times, when music has been handed over, bound and gagged, to the forces of so-called progress.

Finally a few observations on the subject of performance. Our only hope of salvation, a return to the inspiration that comes from the living masterpieces of music (the sole justification for the existence of our musical life, even though few of these masterpieces are from the present age), is all too often stultified by bad performances. The public's attitude in this regard is a strange one. Technical shortcomings, however minor, are mercilessly criticized, whereas desultory or shamelessly distorted performances are accepted without demur.

But on closer inspection, and leaving aside explanations in terms of personal inadequacy, conceit or ostentation, which play their part here as everywhere else, this circumstance seems deeply rooted in the general artistic conditions of the age. We are the same people as performers that we are as creators; we both produce and reproduce; the currents, trends and dangers characteristic of the music of our own time reveal themselves in the way we regard the music of other ages. The inability to feel the fundamental emotional content of a work through its entire course, from beginning to end, is at its most glaringly obvious in those works of whose living example we stand in greatest need today. It is those works that receive the worst performances because they are the very ones that make the greatest spiritual demands on the performer.

Proof of this can be found everywhere, most frequently in performances of the Classics – Bach, and especially Beethoven. There are two broad approaches. One is the 'historical' approach

– that is to say, these works are seen as belonging to an historical period which is over and done with and has no direct relevance to the present age. After hearing a work performed in accordance with such a view, we find ourselves left with not the slightest doubt that it has indeed no relevance to the present age. It has that kind of slick elegance against which Wagner protested and which appears to be enjoying a revival today. Any passionate outbursts that might be considered to be in bad taste are studiously avoided, as is any appeal to present-day emotions and expectations. As a result all expressive emotion is effectively banished from the performance.

The other approach is to thrust one's own personality to the fore and seek, as a modern man, to turn the Classics into modern works. Here, by means of all kinds of espressivo techniques, and in a characteristically modern urge to pack as much emotion into each individual moment as possible, one can see even more starkly how ill-equipped we are for our task.

In both cases the reason is the same – the inability to identify the emotional sources in this great music, that power of emotion and expression that flows through and permeates every part of the living organisms that are these works. One can imagine how great would be the new significance which both the work as a whole and its constituent parts, the one aspect linked to the other, would gain if our situation were properly understood.

13 Open Letter to Dr Joseph Goebbels

Dear Herr Reichsminister:

In view of my many years in public life and of my spiritual links with the music of my native Germany I am taking the liberty of drawing your attention to certain events which have recently taken place in the musical life of our country and which, in my view, have no necessary connection with the restoration of our national honour, which we all welcome with great joy and gratitude.

My feelings are those of a musician, an artist. It is the function of art and artists to unite, not to divide. The only dividing-line I am prepared to acknowledge is that which separates good art from bad art. But whereas a line is being drawn today, a rigid line of ruthless theoretical principle, between Jews and non-Jews, even though the political conduct of those affected has not given any ground for complaint, that other, ultimately so vital and decisive line that separates good and bad is being largely ignored.

Contemporary musical life, which has been made to suffer as a result of the world economic crisis, of the inroads made by radio and other pressures, cannot withstand any further experiments. Music cannot be rationed like the other necessities of life – bread, potatoes and the rest. If concerts have nothing to offer, people will simply stay away. The question of quality is therefore not a theoretical one but one of sheer survival.

If the campaign against the Jews is directed principally against those rootless and sterile performers who are out to impress through *Kitsch*, empty virtuosity and the like, then it is entirely justified. One cannot be too rigorous in one's opposition to such people and the spirit they represent – a spirit, incidentally, which is by no means confined to them.

But if this campaign is aimed against genuine artists, it is against the interests of our cultural life. Wherever it may be, true artists are far too rare for any country to be able to afford to dispense with their services without damaging their own culture.

It must therefore be firmly stated that men like Bruno Walter, Klemperer, Reinhardt[1] and others must be allowed to continue to express themselves through their art.

I repeat: let our opposition be directed against those rootless representatives of a subversive spirit of trivialization and destruction but not against the genuine artist, who, however one assesses his art, is a creator and helps, as such, in the work of reconstruction.

It is in this spirit that I appeal to you, in the name of German music, not to allow things to happen which it might prove impossible to undo.

I remain, Sir, your most obedient servant,

Wilhelm Furtwängler

14 Form and Chaos

Musical life today is characterized by a massive increase in theorizing and a corresponding decline in practical music-making. In fact we have almost reached the point where a composer scarcely dares to write a note without seeking justification in some fashionable ideology, or in some scheme or system on which he can call to prove his credentials as a genuinely 'contemporary' composer.

This need not automatically be a disadvantage. In past ages, when musical composition was more 'natural', composer and listener were linked one to the other by a kind of common *Weltanschauung*. But today the centre of gravity has shifted, and it is as though the music is now only there to serve as a kind of illustration to the corresponding ideological superstructure, which is regarded as the main object of the exercise. As far as I can see, the basic question as to what extent the music actually does correspond to the ideology on which it rests, is hardly ever posed. What is discussed is not the music but the direction in which it is going. As a result we have two kinds of music today – one that is reviewed in journals, and one that is actually played.

An example will show what I mean. Arthur Schnabel was not only an outstanding pianist but also of considerable importance as a composer.[1] He was a masterly interpreter of the Classics – Mozart, Beethoven, Schubert etc. But as far as the public was concerned, his repertoire came to an end with Brahms; hardly ever did he play anything later than Brahms, and one might have assumed that he was one of those oriented entirely towards the past, a man out of tune with the modern world.

But Schnabel was also a composer. And once he had discovered his own style, he proved to belong to the radical, progressive camp, as 'atonal' as any Schoenberg. The public did not esteem his compositions as they did his piano-playing but he confidently continued composing undeterred, remaining faithful to himself and to his own standards. For whatever one thinks of his works, they are not those of an amateur.

How can we reconcile these extremes – a man at one moment a passionate spokesman for the values of the past, at the next a composer of totally radical persuasion? When I once asked him about this glaring contradiction, he replied: 'I compose like Mozart'. Seeing my surprise, he quickly added: 'But with less talent, of course. What I mean is that the process of composition goes on in my mind in much the same way as it did in Mozart's – that is to say, freely, fluently, naturally, unburdened by reflectivity'.

But is this answer of Schnabel's not itself a 'reflection?' Is it conceivable that a composer would seek to justify his creative activity by referring to it as 'fluent and natural?' Indeed, does he need to justify it at all? Is it not for the work itself to do this? Has the society towards which a work is directed not the right to an opinion? Or are modern works no longer directed towards society?

When we look at the matter more closely, one fact strikes us. Schnabel never played one of his own works in public. He did nothing to further the career of Schnabel the composer – that he left to others. One might wonder at first whether he was perhaps over-sensitive, too diffident to thrust himself into the limelight. But this was not the reason. He made a distinction between creator and interpreter, even in himself. He once told me that during the interval of a pianoforte recital he was giving in a small American town, a man came rushing into the artists' room and cried: 'Either you are lying today or you were lying two weeks ago, when we had to listen to your compositions!' When I asked him how he had responded, Schnabel answered with a grin: 'Maybe I was lying both times!' This was, of course, basically a reply designed to get rid of the troublesome questioner. But even so, if it was meant to be the truth – and why should it not have been, coming from a creative artist – then Schnabel would have been prepared to stand by what he said.

Do not misunderstand me. Schnabel was in no way being dishonest. Indeed, we must be grateful to him for having had the self-confidence not to shamefacedly try and conceal the yawning gap between Schnabel the pianist and Schnabel the composer but to openly acknowledge it. In other words, he was what he was.

This one example puts into particularly stark relief a problem which seems to me very much of our time, and which Schnabel, in his unquestionable sincerity, forces us to confront. Let us start with the problem of Schnabel the composer. As he saw it, the naturalness of the creative process was sufficient justification in itself; it required nobody's approval, and he was prepared to forgo any prospect of success for his compositions. Is the world today not full of composers who take this line, writing work after work without heed for what the public – for whom they are writing – think and say, and who, because they compose 'as freely and fluently as Mozart', consider themselves to be creative artists? At the same time the world – not, of course, the unsophisticated public but a large proportion of practising musicians – is inclined, given the frightening lack of objective criteria, to accept at face value what these composers say and to suspect that in everyone who continues to compose unchecked, work after work, there lurks a Mozart or a Schubert. As few of them are interpreters in the same class as Schnabel, the inner contradiction of their position does not become apparent.

But the question now arises, why did an intelligent and un-deniably eminent man like Schnabel distinguish in himself between the creative and the reproductive? Why did not Schnabel the pianist automatically put himself at the service of Schnabel the composer, as would have been natural, and as hitherto had always been the case?

The answer must lie in the character of Schnabel the com-poser. As a pianist, he is no different from other performing artists – with them, he functions within that living context formed by the interplay between the artist and his public. He plays to a body of people, subordinates himself to that body of people (that it is the music of others which he plays, is immaterial).

As a composer, on the other hand, he sits in his ivory tower, indulging his urge, like so many today, to give expression to the movements of his over-sensitive nerves and his sophisticated intellect. This too – and why not? – is a pleasurable activity, and if others take it seriously, so much the better. But it was because he was so totally committed a performer that he did not include his own works, or any by other contemporary com-posers, in his repertoire. As a pianist, playing to a public he knew, he was conscious of standards, of criteria which, as a composer, he could not achieve.

So why did he compose at all? Why are all these people composing today without addressing themselves to a public with whom they could establish an immediate, natural relationship? If Schnabel the composer had done this, he would certainly nct have refrained from performing his own works.

As the composer sees it, the work of art is a living symbol of the sense of one-ness that embraces him and his audience. The knowledge that one will never receive any response from the audience for whom one is actually writing will gradually undermine the will to compose and eventually even the ability to compose. Without the presence of a community, a society in the background, a work of music – a communal work in the truest sense – cannot survive. If there are composers around today – and there are many: Schnabel is not an isolated case – who can go on composing regardless of whether they have listeners or not, maintaining that they are composing for the future, then either we are dealing with a different conception of music and the musician, or the public has changed. At all events there can be no doubt but that there has been a considerable shift in the relationship between composer and public in the twentieth century, more particularly since the beginning of the atonal period. This is admitted both by the public and by composers themselves, who are those most immediately affected.

Who and what is this public? In the sense in which the question is asked, the public forms part of the great 'Thou', the great world outside ourselves, to which the artist addresses his activity.[2] Whether it is a middle-class public or a working-class public is of no account, nor is its nationality. Even a nation ethnically so different from ourselves as the Japanese shows itself responsive to European music today. We are talking here about a public, a body of people who feel as a community and react as a community, not a mass of individuals. This is a significant distinction. Experts have repeatedly discovered, to their surprise, that however mistaken, even stupid an individual's opinions may be, those of the public at large can often be infernally rational and sharp-witted.

Obviously it is the general public that provides the economic foundation for public musical life. Less obvious is what this means for the composer. In the first place the public represents the 'imaginary listener' to whom the composer addresses his message. From the time of Bach this public was a kind of 'supreme court' for composers, the body that upheld certain principles and standards. When theoreticians and critics talk today of the 'rules' of music that they have derived from Bach,

Beethoven, Schubert, Wagner, Brahms etc., we must realize that
all such rules are inconceivable without the existence of a public.
They are like instructions which the composer follows as he
formulates his answer to the question: How do I ensure that I
speak to the public in such clear and precise terms that they
will fully understand my meaning? To this extent one can also
say that the great composers had a big hand in the creation of
their public, however it was constituted. Beethoven is known
to have been consistently critical of the public before whom he
played at his concerts in Vienna, yet it was he, through his
works, particularly his symphonies, who decisively influenced
the whole course of public musical life in the nineteenth century,
helping thereby to actually create that musical life.

Today, however, it is clear that the deep-rooted, if unspoken
mutual confidence which existed between composer and public
in the nineteenth century, despite many conflicts and differences
of opinion, has been shaken. Little is left of that feeling of being
joined together with the public through a bond of spiritual
unity, of trusting the public and serving it, which Wagner still
had, and Strauss too. The modern composer now confronts his
listeners with a set of demands; no longer does he subordinate
himself to their wishes but expects them to submit to his authority. He has ceased to be in the community and is now above
it. Nor does he conceal what he thinks of the public, namely
very little. What had previously been an ideal, all-embracing
relationship has been reduced to the level of practical expedi-
ency. He seeks to influence the public – whom he needs at least
on economic grounds – by patronizing and browbeating them,
and he floods the market with a mass of propaganda, paraded
with all the ostentation typical of publicity campaigns, on behalf
of modern music and modern musicians.

How modest and unassuming he is! Does he really rate it a
success if his propaganda manages to bludgeon the public into
silence? Does he really consider what is in the newspapers to
be more important than what goes on in people's hearts? And
what has an exercise in special pleading to do with art?

In the last analysis what we call the 'public' is in fact beyond
being influenced. One can easily intimidate people or deprive
them of their self-confidence, whereupon they will simply crawl
back into their own shell. But to induce them to find things
attractive which are not to their liking is ultimately impossible
because their decisions are instinctively, unconsciously based on
natural, omnipresent laws within them. What the artist should

seek after, namely a relationship of mutual affection between himself and his public, cannot be created by force, by being patronizing or by belabouring them with theories of this kind or that. The gap between today's avant-garde composers and the general public has certainly not been closing in recent decades (the few exceptions only go to prove the rule). It is no accident that since the beginning of the atonal period no opera has been written which has found its way into the regular repertoire – as *Der Rosenkavalier*, for instance, still managed to do.

Those charged with the task of following these developments, namely historians of music, can give us no information. The passing of perceptive, well-informed value judgements is in any case a matter usually left to later periods, especially as contemporary historiography is always in danger of adopting the clichés of the moment. In fact, a facile, so-called 'historical perspective' has recently become one of the main weapons in the propaganda war. Instant judgements are dispensed: Bartók and Hindemith, for example, notwithstanding the numerous differences between them, are dignified with the title 'modern Classics' and assigned the same importance for our age as Mozart and Beethoven had for theirs. It will be some considerable time before the real history of music in the last fifty years can be written.

The rise of atonality, liberation from what were suddenly felt to be the shackles of tonality, dates from the first decade of the twentieth century. The first shots in the war were fired by Arnold Schoenberg with his totally new, bold, revolutionary pieces in the so-called twelve-tone system of composition.[3] This was not – as it first appeared to be and as many composers themselves believed – an extension of certain already detectable trends but something totally new. By removing the concept of consonance and dissonance and rearranging the musical material in a completely new way, Schoenberg changed the whole process of composition. Hitherto guided by emotion, with the aid of the intellect – though the former always predominated – the process now acquired a theoretical dimension, which showed itself above all in the avoidance of all those tonal associations that had formerly been regarded as natural.

As a consequence, on the one hand the nature of the expressive quality of music changed, setting the listener new and totally unfamiliar tasks. On the other hand the composer acquired a new method of working which appeared to offer him a new freedom, a sudden feeling of release from the 'tyranny' of tonality. This had an intoxicating effect, and it is understandable that considerations of how the public would cope with the new music should be dismissed as unnecessary obstacles, particularly as the historically-based theory that lay at its roots afforded an excellent opportunity for publicizing its cause.

But above all – and this was the nub of the matter – composition became easy again, as in the age of Mozart, in Schnabel's words. Small wonder that the movement spread with such bewildering rapidity. The early works of Hindemith and Křenek, written during the years following the Great War, mark the first climax of atonality.[4] Within the space of a bare ten years the greatest revolution in the history of music had taken place, the emergence of something totally new.

It is a characteristic fact that the full extent of this revolution could only be judged by people who read the press. It was a public revolution. Above all there was a change in the public's attitude towards contemporary composers. In earlier times composers faced considerable difficulties. They had had to engage in the struggle for existence which had characterized the whole of nature from the beginning and in which only the strongest and fittest could expect to survive. The public, the same drowsy, lethargic mass that it had always been, was satisfied with what it knew and loved and had an automatic aversion to anything new. Not only that, but the critics too – who were at that time far closer to the public than they are today and reflected public attitudes more accurately – joined in the chorus of disapproval, frequently, as shown by their verdict on works which subsequently came to be acknowledged as masterpieces, outdoing the public in their hostility. If a particular work or a particular composer did make a mark, then it was the achievement of this work, this composer himself. And what enabled him to make this mark was not propaganda but recognition on the part of the public whom, in spite of their proverbial lethargy, he had succeeded in winning over, using their help to create a new spiritual community of his own. A young composer could not automatically rely on the public's goodwill in those days. They did not feel that they owed him a living, and if his works failed to please, he had little alternative but to throw them on the junk heap.

How different things are today! Young composers are now treated as guarantors of the future, spoilt and pampered at every turn – with one proviso: that they satisfy the ideological demands of the age by writing 'progressive' music that 'points the way forward'. If they fulfil this requirement according to the intellectual precept of the moment, they are admitted to the ranks of those working for the cause of progress. Since there are many such composers around today, the general public has developed something like a feeling of social responsibility towards them, along the lines that one must give the younger generation the opportunity to live and work, since it is they who represent the future and we who must smooth their path.

Thus it is not a question, for the public, of adopting a particular stance in the interests of the future of art in general, or of the future of 'modern man', but of promoting the interests of a particular group of composers, of making it possible for them to carry on their work within the framework of a particular system, a particular theory, of providing a work pattern. The public takes second place. At the same time 'modern man' has to understand that it is not the function of music to speak to his 'soul' – this is just a hangover from the romantic past.

What a difference from the situation of the young composer in earlier ages! As to those not fortunate enough to be acknowledged by the public as guarantors of the future but content just to go on writing music – maybe very good music – about such I have nothing to say. However good they may be, today they are deader than dead.

But what about the others, those who are encouraged as representatives of the prevailing ideology? If we look at their position objectively, the encouragement they receive seems to have had the very opposite effect to that which the earnest and committed proponents of that ideology might have expected. Since the composer no longer has to establish his credentials, so to speak, with each successive work but only has to attach himself to a specific trend in order to be taken seriously, there arises an enervating, nerveless hothouse atmosphere which is the very reverse of beneficial to his development in the long run. They say that hares which are kept in captivity, away from the threat of attack by their natural enemies like eagles and foxes, gradually lose their alertness and adaptability. The same thing happens to artists. Wherever one looks, one finds that under the influence of the modern desire to protect and assist our poor composers, their works have become not better but worse. The group shields the individual, for whom it becomes more important to demonstrate his allegiance to the group than to justify himself directly to the public, whom he is extremely reluctant to acknowledge as his equal.

In the past it was not so. Then it was always the individual who confronted his fellow-men and won them over. Mozart, Beethoven, Schubert, Wagner – none of them represented a 'trend'. Today, in contrast, the individual seeks safety in numbers. Thomas Mann took pride in the fact that he had never belonged to a coterie or subscribed to a specific *Weltanschauung*; he valued his 'splendid isolation', and rightly so. The true composers who are still among us, those who have given us truly living works, have all been lone figures in this mould.

Many reasons can be adduced for the domination of such groups. There is, for example, a highly efficient organization sustained by the wealth of big music publishers, with all modern resources at its disposal; intent on selling their wares, they have taken it upon themselves not only to disparage genuine composers who are working along different lines but recently even to play down the importance of the great music of the past, the life-blood of our musical world, which had come to be regarded as offering unwelcome competition. Is this the pass to which we have come in the emasculation and degradation of modern man? Does that public on which the great European music of recent centuries depended no longer exist?

Of one thing I am certain. If composers no longer conceive of the public as a source of divine judgement, as the voice of nature, as the spokesman for mankind, and if the God-given partnership, the voluntary community of affection, between artist and public no longer exists, then we are facing the final collapse of everything that has hitherto been called art, everything that has been truly creative.

I have always suspected that behind this entire sequence of extraordinary developments there is a hidden force at work, a higher power, and that what we are witnessing cannot be explained in its own terms but must be seen as symbolizing something more profound.

Travellers who have camped at night in the African jungle record how overwhelmed they were by the unbridled forces of nature. It was as though all the gates of hell had been unloosed, the roar of a thousand voices proclaiming the fearful power of primeval creation – in a word, chaos, which is for modern man a strange, uncanny experience, to put it no higher.

A similar feeling is said to be induced by the sound of drums in the African jungle, pounding out their message from far and near in never-ending ostinato rhythms the whole night long. Here it is not the variety of sounds but the interminable, merciless thudding that has such an elemental effect on the listener, an effect incomparable to anything in European experience.

This chaos, absorbed, as it were, in its 'raw' acoustical state, appears to have influenced the music of modern Europe. Let us recall the case of Arthur Schnabel, who as a pianist lived within the great tradition of the past but as a composer subscribed to the modern cult of irrationalism. Had the intellectual theorizing which swept over the musical scene at the beginning of the twentieth century, replacing the tonal order of things with auditory chaos, really been only a short-lived, alien influence, an antidote would have long since been found for the poison that it injected into the hitherto healthy body of European music. The whole movement would have come to an end. But it has not. Modern man – at least in part – must have developed an affinity to chaos which was not previously there. This, and nothing else, is what is new in modern art.

This leaves us with a series of further questions. Why is this so? Why did chaos not play the role in earlier times that it evidently plays today? Has mankind undergone a fundamental change in recent years? Is it connected in some way with the two World Wars that we have been through?

We need to think very clearly and objectively about these matters. Let me recapitulate. In the light of modern music we must assume that many people are more susceptible to irrational influences today than they were, say, at the beginning of the century. It is a feature of the consciousness of modern man that not only has his art not lost its affinity to chaos but constantly reaffirms it, emphasizing that it no longer owes allegiance to what we are accustomed to regard as the opposite of chaos, namely what is rational and accountable. It is the rational principle, as embedded in the system of tonality, which is under attack and from which men anxiously shrink, even at the risk of jettisoning the positive aspects of tonality, such as its capacity to sustain formal structures. Fear of reason and being in thrall to chaos are only a step apart – indeed, in the profoundest sense they are one and the same. So how has this come to be such a prominent characteristic of modern man?

Histories of music, as I said above, tell us nothing. Historians even appear unaware of certain vital facts which ought to occupy their attention. For example, why is it that for a whole generation, since the end of the First World War, there has in

fact been no development in music? Those years marked the
onset of atonality. Schoenberg's theories and the works of
Bartók, Stravinsky, Hindemith and others belong to this period.[5]
But the new freedom gained at that time has not been carried
any further. Attempts were made to encapsulate this freedom
in systems: Schoenberg led the way with his twelve-tone system
and others followed. In the meantime there have also been
individual efforts to overcome the situation, for example, by
marrying the old and the new. But none of this has altered the
fundamental situation. Development has stopped.

In keeping with the way people see themselves and their art
today, attention has become increasingly concentrated on the
'material' of music. Whatever 'development' there may have
been has not been connected with the progress of man himself
but with independent technical advances in the field of harmony, rhythm etc. In other words, it is the methodology that
has developed, not the soul of the artist whose emotions the
methodology is there to help express. Historians laid down the
precise year up to which tonal harmony could legitimately be
used to serve functional ends, and the precise year when this
would become no longer feasible. The closer this whole line
of development came to its inevitable termination, the more
desperately it clung to one dominating idea – progress, progress
at any price. This was all the more peculiar because it is obvious
that all progress based on matter and its exploitation must one
day come to an end.

For all that, the battle between atonal and tonal music,
between the New Music and the European music of the last
three hundred years, shows no signs of losing its vehemence.
The weapons may change but the rival trenches remain in the
same position. In spite of massive publicity campaigns the New
Music has not succeeded in gaining itself a larger, more depend-
able public but neither has it forfeited its socio-ethical appeal to
any degree.

There must, it seems, be some profound reason why this
situation, which in the long run is intolerable for all concerned,
is allowed to persist. Is it perhaps inevitable? Are we maybe
observing a necessary concomitant of the development of
modern life, welcomed by some, resented by others?

Human intelligence, in so far as it has been directed towards
the exploitation of the physical world, has developed more consistently and more rapidly than at any time in the previous
history of mankind. Much of the world has been tamed, subju-

gated by the exercise of scientific reason and the forces of technology. But it is not possible to reveal part of the world which has hitherto been shrouded in darkness without accepting the consequences of this revelation. And we are only beginning to realize what those consequences are.

Man's life is lived between reason and chaos, between the physical world that he has subordinated to his own purposes and the world of the irrational, the unfathomable, the unknowable – God. Having mastered the physical world and removed from it most of its irrational content, we become intoxicated with the sense of our own power. Whereupon the chaos that we have driven out of the front door insinuates itself into the house from the rear. For this chaos is a part of ourselves. Indeed, it is this very preponderance of the critical intellect and the power of reason which, in the moment when our victory over the external world seems to be sealed, instils in us modern Europeans a sudden paralysing fear of being left alone with our reason – or, put another way, of finding ourselves locked in the prison of our own rational intelligence.

This is the position from which we need to understand the fascination with chaos that runs through the whole development of modern music. This chaos, stark and uncompromising, is felt to offer a liberation, a deliverance, while there is an over-sensitive reaction against anything, real or imagined, that evokes memories of one's reason, of which one has had more than one's fill. It is also the position from which to approach the twelve-tone system of Schoenberg, which as an auditory experience conveys the spirit of chaos but as a method of composition is the epitome of the world of modern science, the most highly rationalized system imaginable. Chaos and Reason – the Scylla and Charibdis between which modern man is buffeted to and fro.

Apart from the numerous areas of detail in which this predicament can be observed, the broad outlines of the situation indicate another basic truth, namely, that behind all this lies, not one single, universal, all-embracing development but only a partial development. It is not the public as a whole that reacts in this way, not 'modern man' who is tortured by this dilemma but quite evidently only a particular set of intellectuals.

The concert-going public brings its own influence to bear on musical life in that it is present and pays for that privilege. We have a better chance of defining the characteristics of modern man – whom the public represents – through observing those who attend musical events than those who, for instance, visit exhibitions or picture galleries, where the public is a more or less anonymous entity. And here we find ourselves facing the incontrovertible fact that there are elements in this public that do not share the general view. It is a situation riven with dis-agreements – a crisis situation.

To deny this, claiming that the current state of affairs is per-fectly normal, even logical, and that twelve-tone music expresses the soul of modern man in the same sense in which Mozart and Beethoven expressed the soul of their age, is a striking example of the extent to which we are 'locked in the prison of our rational intelligence', as I put it above. Linked to this is the urge to anticipate future developments and influence their course. Also linked to this is a conviction that it is more impor-tant to woo the future than to satisfy the present – that our responsibility towards this future is so great that all prospects of pleasure in the here and now must be relegated to second place. Indeed, nothing is more calculated to perpetuate the crisis than the aesthetic principles of the New Music, with which we have been bombarded for over a generation. That genuine development is not sought after, not planned but experienced as an injunction of fate; that one can only serve the future by fulfilling the needs of the present, i.e. that only a work which has a relevance for the age in which it was written can be of any significance for the future – thoughts such as these appear to have all but disappeared.

What a grotesque situation! Here are creative artists allowing themselves to be dictated to by critics, theoreticians and his-torians – one only has to glance at any music journal or listen to the statements of contemporary composers in order to see this. Is this not the most vivid illustration, the most convincing evidence one could ask for, that we and our whole philosophy of art are shackled and fettered like no age before us? In order to be relieved of our responsibility towards the present, we are taking refuge in the future. Wittingly or unwittingly we are being intimidated by slogans like 'progress' and 'evolution', which would be in a position to destroy the whole of European musical life if – and only if – the New Music were the only music there is. That is what the New Music itself believes, of course, because, being blinkered by its own ideas, it believes in principles and programmes. As cannot be repeated too often, however, what matters is not principles and programmes – the more attractive they are, the less they usually have to say about the real state of affairs – but to what extent such theoretical statements are vindicated by the music itself.

The genuine music of an age is a creative fact, not a matter of ideology. It is from the music, the created music, that everything starts. Only then comes theoretical interpretation, which, if it is to have any meaning at all, must keep strictly to reality, to the created work – a reflection of the original, as it were. If it loses that contact with reality, it loses its validity. This only becomes clear after a while, however. To start with, it even makes itself out to be more important, acting vicariously on behalf of the music, which gets pushed into the background. It puts out the 'thought-content' of the music in advance, lays down its programme.

The longer this analytical process continues, the more the actual creative process loses the strength and directness of its appeal. The composer no longer addresses the public face-to-face but comes to rely on the programme, the ideology to help make his music intelligible and acceptable. The direct artist-public relationship no longer has the power it once had.

There is, however, a law that the public will only fully accept what is really written for the public. The relationship between artist and public exists, like any relationship, by mutual consent. This is precisely what the famous words mean that Beethoven put at the head of his greatest work, the Missa Solemnis: '*Von Herzen – möge es zu Herzen gehen*' ('From the heart – may it reach to the heart'). What is not written for people will not be accepted by people. If so many composers today think it their business to write for critics rather than for people, they will no doubt earn the critics' gratitude but they must not be surprised if they are given a cool reception by the public.

Real composers speak as directly and as exclusively to a living public as possible. That is what Bach, Mozart, Beethoven and all the other great composers have done, right down to our own time. And if virtuosi like Liszt and Tchaikovsky composed for the 'masses', as people sometimes sneer, that is not to be held against them. It is not the artist's relationship to the public as such that characterizes the artist and gives him his sense of direction but the nature of this relationship, i.e. the nature of the public that he addresses. Every artist speaks to a different section of the public according to the nature of his personality; which section he chooses gives us an insight into that personality. By the same token it is a reflection on his ability and his powers if he lacks the courage to confront his public other than with the assistance of critical principles and theories.

The accord between composer and theorist, a marriage arrived at by mutual consent, has created a situation of reversed roles, a vicious circle which we cannot afford to ignore. As the composer cannot, *qua* composer, stand on his own feet, and has no wish to do so, he needs the help of theory. And since the theorist, for his part, no longer feels himself to be just a reflection of the composer as a creative artist, he steps outside his proper area of competence and lays down his wishes and requirements, in the belief that he is being of assistance to the composer. This gives the theorist an importance hitherto unheard-of – less, however, in the form of critical explanation and support (for which artists are always grateful) than as an agent of propaganda.

Obviously any such propaganda is at pains to present its own arguments as reflecting the true musical life of contemporary man. But the question immediately arises, who is this 'contemporary man' whose interests these propagandists so brazenly claim to represent?

I would define 'contemporary man' as man in the actual form in which he confronts us today. Those whom the great artists of the eighteenth and nineteenth century addressed, those who sustained the activities of these artists, were similarly the 'contemporary men' of their age. 'Contemporary man', or 'modern man', if you will, can only be understood in his entirety. He is for the artist of today what the public was for the great masters of the past – the 'Thou', a partner united in the bond of love, the bosom in which creation is nurtured. He is a richer, more comprehensive entity than modern aestheticians, victims of a facile belief in progress, would have us think. They, for their part, as solemn and narrowminded as they are presumptuous and intolerant, appear to believe that they can predict the course of the future, can tell us what fate has in store. The real 'modern man', to the extent that he is a creative being, is rich and abundant, varied and versatile, whereas the propagandists regard him not only as being a poverty-stricken creature but as actually wanting to be such. How rich was musical life at the beginning of the century – Richard Strauss, Pfitzner, Max Reger, Mahler, Schoenberg, Debussy, Ravel, Honegger, Stravinsky, Bartók, the young Hindemith! How numerous were the names, how varied the personalities, how manifold the ways of handling the material of music! In my father's house are many mansions, as the Bible has it.

And what about today? Are not the few composers whose names recur over and over again in our music festivals in process of becoming more and more like each other, more and more uniform in their attitudes towards the task of composition?

Those in our society who are preoccupied with thoughts of the future, those intent on peddling their programmes, naturally maintain that they are the true spokesmen for modern man. The first thing to say to this is that modern man is not some ideal vision, a creature as we would like him to be – a product of propaganda, in a word – but a physical fact. Reality in the round consists not only of what one would like to be but above all of what one actually is. The resistance of the public – a resistance responsible for the flood of propaganda that has descended upon us – itself proves that the public, i.e. modern man, possesses other characteristics than those which the propagandists have chosen to emphasize.

There are certain different types of modern man that we can distinguish. First come those who are aware of the uncertainty of speculating about the future and aware of the limits of human reason. This knowledge is innate, not acquired – it is fundamental, instinctive, natural knowledge. Such men also see the inexhaustible riches of nature and do not lose sight of human emotions in the general enthusiasm for theories and doctrines. Many musicians belong to this type, signally those great performers who for professional reasons alone could not afford to ignore the vital emotional aspect of their activity and who reject outright all manufactured, artificial, 'unheard' music. In the same company are scholars and philosophers far too absorbed with the problem of the limits of human reason ever to fall into the trap of over-estimating that faculty.

Alongside this philosophical type I would set the man who lives beyond art and knowledge, the man who faces life as a clear, open, direct experience. Far from being interested in furthering his 'development' through moral renunciation or some intellectual exercise, he makes the frank, irresistible demand to be allowed to experience art directly, to recognize it as a part of himself and – sinister word! – to enjoy it. He does not have preconceived notions about what art should be but accepts it with an open mind, above all retaining the determination and the strength to remain the person that he is, to be his own man.

So our 'modern man', in the context of music today, is compounded of three different types. Firstly, there is the 'propagandist', as we called him, the man with a fixed purpose. Secondly, there is the man who looks more deeply into the matter and views the contrasts and conflicts from above – the man of awareness, as one might call him. And thirdly he who approaches the question naively, naturally, as one with his own inalienable feelings – the man of emotion. These are the three types who go into the making of modern man, the true representative of the state of music today, the true judge of what music shall exist and what shall not, the true arbiter of the course that the music of the future shall follow.

It needs to be stressed that these three types are rarely to be found in their pure form. In practice what we encounter are usually mixed forms, the elements in which each and every one of us has in himself – some to a greater extent, some to a lesser. The proportions, moreover, can also fluctuate: a person may tend to represent one type at one time and another type at a different time. Expressed in these basic terms, however, these three types make up the ethos of modern man.

Understandably, it is the first type, the man with a purpose, that is the most prominent, because he is intent on influencing the course of our musical life. Chief among them are critics, working through journals, radio and other media. I well remember overhearing a conversation between Richard Strauss and Joseph Goebbels, the Nazi Minister of Propaganda, in which Strauss, regarded for decades as the leader of the progressives, passionately defended the public's right to listen to what it wanted and to make up its own mind, and refused to countenance the infringement of this right by any third party.

But the astute propagandist of today, of course, has learned his trade from Goebbels rather than from Strauss. Active and aggressive, he seeks the company only of those of his own kind, refusing to acknowledge the rights of those of different persuasion. The only thought in his mind is that of subjugation. He is concerned neither with emotion nor with understanding but solely with power. The will to power – that is his driving force. And as Nietzsche foresaw, that means power over nature and eventually power over men. Small wonder that he has succeeded in dominating our musical life to an extent inconceivable in earlier times, when such men were far rarer and less sophisticated. And how determinedly, how ruthlessly he wields this power! Everything is planned, down to the smallest detail.

Not the slightest doubt is allowed to cross his mind. Concepts like fairness and propriety, upheld by men like Richard Strauss, which would ensure that composers of different persuasion, whose music one perhaps did not understand, were still given the chance to prove their quality in public – such concepts are beyond his comprehension. And those who do not share his prejudices and his blinkered views are simply ignored, or ridiculed, or demolished.

It has probably always been the case that those who hold power are those who want to hold it. At the moment these figures in our musical life may be able to impede the natural process by which music of real quality will rise to the surface but they cannot determine the future course of music. For this future is also the future of modern man himself. With stubborn persistence these propagandists, as we have called them, have maintained that they and modern man are one and the same. Why? Because it is on this conviction, held both by themselves and by others, that they depend for their very existence. But in spite of this – indeed, because of it – the situation is not like this. Once and for all we must recognize the vicious circle that links ideological hubris and abstract, intellectual, un-heard music. We shall never escape from this vicious circle unless and until we resolve that, instead of paying homage to some speculative belief in the future, we shall be ourselves, shall turn our minds to our own present and restore our faith in life.

What the propagandist lacks is the 'Thou', the world of his fellow-men. In his search for boundless power, as we have said, he can recognize only himself and those of like mind. Bereft of any sense of awe and wonder at the outside world, he is mesmerized by the power of his own all-conquering intelligence. It does not matter whether one calls this outside world 'God', 'Nature', or both – what matters is that it is there. It is vital for us to realize what is happening. As life becomes increasingly subject to the processes of quantification and mensurability, all the experiences and emotions which are not amenable to such treatment become pushed into the background and ultimately disappear altogether. Nature, the great 'Thou' of earlier ages, exists only to be conquered and exploited, and is thus no longer a true 'Thou'. All the emotions evoked in such a context – reverence, wonder, contemplation, serenity, to say nothing of religious values such as prayer and worship – gradually lose their power and their validity and eventually fade away. Objections are raised to the 'hero worship' characteristic of earlier ages – in reality simply a worship of the forces of divine nature embodied in the personality of the great man – and in its place proud claims are made for the advance of historical conscious-ness, far removed from anything that smacks of the outdated romanticism of the nineteenth century.

For music this absence of the 'Thou' spells disaster. It means the end of the development of aesthetic form as we know it. For form cannot emerge and evolve without the interplay – the struggle, even – between composer and public, between the creator and the world in and for which he creates.

I have no wish to engage here in a discussion of the nature of aesthetic form. It is a mystery. Those who have experienced this mystery for themselves have no problem in unravelling it but it is immensely difficult to put into words. I will only repeat: without the reality of the 'I' and 'Thou' situation, i.e. without the acknowledgement by the artist of a human community that he addresses, the notion of aesthetic form is meaningless. From the standpoint of modern man, with his peculiar attraction to chaos, form provides a way of overcoming, exorcising, control-ling this chaos, starting with the vision of the work as a whole and reaching down to every little detail. Brought thus under the control of the formal principle, chaos can be found equally in the overall vision of a symphony and in the concentrated moment of an individual melody from that symphony. In this sense, there is more real 'chaos' in a single melody from Bizet's *Carmen* than in numerous longwinded modern works.

But if we attempt to circumvent the process by which aesthetic form is achieved – whether because, as modern men, we are too anxious to grasp this chaos in its pure, naked form, or because, no longer having a 'Thou', we are no longer able to give chaos a name, a form – if, as I say, we attempt to approach this chaos directly, then we shall always produce the same disastrous result, namely chaos. Art which has not been sub-jected to the formative process also contains chaos but it is not the chaos of a melody from *Carmen* – it is something pallid, something noncommittal. It is irrational to such an extent that, in contrast to the art of earlier periods, it disguises the creative personality rather than reveals it – which is one of the reasons, incidentally, why such masses of music are being written today.

At the same time it is a strangely unreal form of art, even if, for a moment, it appears to offer salvation to a particular type of person at a particular phase in his development. As an art, music assumes the existence of a public, a community. Not that the visual arts or literature do not also make this assumption – but in musical life this public has a direct, virtually personified role to play. Painters and sculptors today can sometimes be heard to maintain with pride and satisfaction that they can function independently of the market, i.e. of the public. For a musician this is impossible. A composer who claims to be free of the need for public success emerges as an over-zealous individualist. The fact that music still assumes the presence of a public has been our strongest protection from the danger of severing the bond that joins us musicians to mankind, to nature, to God.

It is the consciousness of the vital importance of this bond, of this community, that has been at the root of these reflections. The essential factor is and remains Man. Behind all Art is Man. It is Man that Art expresses, and Art is Man, who creates it. As long as my faith in Man persists – not that tense, bigoted, hide-bound creature locked in the prison of his own thought-processes but modern man in all his breadth and depth, in the intensity of his love and the compass of his knowledge – I shall not allow my faith and confidence in his Art to perish.

15 'Greatness is Simplicity'

Where this well-known saying comes from, I do not know. It is, however, one of those maxims that appear to present no problems to the unsophisticated, natural man but arouse doubts in the minds of our intellectuals. Why should great achievements be 'simple'? Surely that cannot apply to the modern age of technology, when endless new discoveries and inventions show the world to be anything but 'simple'? We have learned how to build machines of an unbelievable complexity – is there not something great about this? In fact, is this not the source of our greatness?

Actually this is a motto that belongs to the realm of the arts, and was coined in an age that still counted the arts among its most vital possessions. When we glibly say today that we have entered the age of technology – or, more accurately, the age of science, to which we owe the advance of technology – it sounds at first like an obvious statement. But we are unaware of how profound the inner, spiritual transformation is that this statement conceals. Or, put more precisely, this transformation has not yet impressed itself so firmly on our minds for the very reason that it is so profound.

'Greatness is simplicity' pertains to the world of the arts because, in the first place, the word 'simple' assumes the existence of an entity, a whole. The whole in this sense is not only a separate, independent part of the world but also, as such, a reflection of this world in its wholeness. It was in the whole that Goethe identified the presence of the Demonic.[1] The inorganic world is ignorant of such a concept of wholeness because that world is infinite, has no limits. The term wholeness in our sense is relevant only by virtue of the fact that we, as human beings, are part of organic life. We think as organisms, we feel as organisms, and every organism – every plant, every animal – constitutes for us something whole. Every whole, however, must be 'simple' in its own way, and by seeing it as a whole

160

we are making it simple. Thus 'Greatness is Simplicity' also appears to signify that what we feel to be great is at the same time part of the organic world.

But this, at least in the eyes of the modern-day world, is not correct. As well as the organic world, which alone governed the thinking of man in the Middle Ages, for example, we now have to accommodate the inorganic world, the cosmos, which science has made part of our experience. Science, which has so radically transformed the external world, is playing an ever greater part in our mental life and is on the point of having a profound effect on those aspects of our life which we have always regarded as the most vitally human – our art and our religion. This gives rise to problems for art and for artistic life unknown to man over the previous millennia of his existence, problems which it is the obligation of artists to confront before it is too late.

The artist lives by creating, by giving expression in organic, finite form, in work upon work, to the infinite power of creative nature. What he requires is, on the one hand the intuitive vision of a 'whole', on the other hand the tenacity to give this vision flesh and blood, to convert it into a modern experience of reality. But science pays scant heed to the artistic intuition that gives birth to the individual work of art, still less to the artist's fanatical attempts to give form and reality to his vision. For science is not concerned with the specific and the particular but with the general and the typical. It sees art as an over-estimation of outer appearances, an over-indulgence in the sensory attractions of physical life. Whereas the artist must avoid at all costs everything that distracts him from solving the problems presented by the individual work on which he is engaged – must avoid anything that might tempt him to take refuge in 'routine' – the scientist is set on discovering what it is that links and underlies the manifestations of the individual and the particular. For the scientist it is not a question of being 'tempted' to seek the general – it is his duty to do so. It is what he calls his 'method'.

Nietzsche was the first to recognize the full seriousness of the problem. In his early days, while he was still under the influence of Wagner, he acknowledged the necessity of art and with it the validity of external appearances, for this was a period when music, at least, still had real power. Later he began to become conscious of his role as the philosopher of the rising age of science. His later attacks on Wagner owed their effect to the fact that they were in accord with the spirit of the times, whereas Wagner, lonely artist in an age about to come under the domination of science, was basically out of tune with that age.

Today the victory of scientific thought seems assured. But let there be no misunderstanding. Scientific thought, in the sense in which I am using the term, is only indirectly related to the recent great advances in our knowledge of the world, which depend as much on the faculty of intuition as do the arts. I am thinking more of science as understood in the middle of the nineteenth century. And by contrasting scientific thought with artistic thought, I am not thinking of generalized, abstract truths, with which we are being swamped at the present time, especially in Central Europe. These are of little value. What I have in mind is two fundamentally different attitudes towards the world. These two attitudes are rarely found in their pure form; most people have them in varying proportions, according to their temperament and their gifts, as well as to their experiences and, not least, their character. All those involved in music, whether domestic or public, partake of both attitudes. It is in the nature of the complexity of artistic life that it should be so. It was so in the ages in which great works were produced. Every artist must be guided, among other things, by a sense of direction, the product of his intellect. But *nota bene* – 'among other things'. This is the crux of the matter. For the crisis that faces musical life today has arisen because the 'scientific' mode of thought has come to predominate at the expense of everything else.

There are a good many things I could say about this on the basis of my own experience, for when I started my career, this development had not yet begun. The first decades of the twentieth century stood in the shadow of the great musical moments of the preceding centuries. Everything was flourishing in the musical garden of Europe – although it did have its weeds. And there were prominent new names – Debussy, Ravel, Reger, Pfitzner, the young Stravinsky. But today things have changed, and for the composer who wants to keep 'abreast of his time' the path is becoming ever narrower, ever more barren.

Nor is this a change that concerns only composers. Performers are equally affected. It used to be a conductor's or pianist's aim to give as vivid an interpretation as possible of the great works in the repertoire. People still had a profound faith in these works. It was still an age of hero-worship, which enlightened thinkers today look down upon as *passé*. In those days it was the pianist's aim to bring to the works of, say, Beethoven all the clarity, the warmth, the directness, the formal discipline and the grandeur that they demanded. The average performance of today makes one wonder whether such works have suddenly lost their interest for modern players. Yet the works have not changed, nor has the broad mass of the public. So what has happened? Could it really be that current attitudes, whose influence none of us can totally escape, are having such an effect?

I would explain the situation in this way. Formerly Beethoven – one could name many others in his place – was seen as a great composer, a divine creator, a source of divine grace, who awoke in us the consciousness of belonging to the world of divine nature that surrounded us. He was what might be called a fragment of religious reality. This is what he signified for Wagner, for Brahms, for Mahler – but much less so today. One sign of this is that present-day audiences accept without demur performances of Beethoven which in earlier times would have been frankly impossible. Beethoven is now seen primarily as one of the 'First Viennese School', an historical phenomenon with an undoubted importance in his day but no longer of much immediate relevance to us in the present age. That there was an historical context to Beethoven's music was something that we were always aware of. But that that was the most important aspect of his work – indeed, that it was all that there was to him – was something we did not know.

The reason for all this lies deeper. Today people have come to realize the importance of the historical perspective, the overview, for our understanding of reality. We are constantly striving to take a bird's eye view of things. Rather than experience a work of art directly, surrendering ourselves to its message, we set out to try and understand it, explain it, thus bring it under our control. This is the method of modern science.

So what consequences does this have for us musicians today? Since musical life is a whole, and comprises not only how we compose today but also how we see and experience the music of the past, the consequences can be felt everywhere. Our attitudes have changed out of all recognition without our realizing it. I spoke a moment ago about performing Beethoven. In performances today the public looks not so much for an interpretation that goes to the heart of the work and its message as for one that follows certain general guidelines based on the abstract, speculative tendencies fashionable at the present time. 'Classical' works must be played in an appropriate 'period style' – which can mean anything except personally coming to grips with those works as a man of the twentieth century. 'Appropriate' means 'according to the age in which the works were written'. The focus of attention is not the personality of the composer Ludwig van Beethoven but what makes him a member of the 'First Viennese School', what he has in common with his age. (In Beethoven, moreover, we sense the gradual encroachment of that subjective, Romantic tendency which is part of the nine-teenth century and which is regarded with such suspicion today.)

Numerous questions that used to be seen as major problems in Beethoven's works – highly structured works that are full of problems – now appear to have suddenly solved themselves. They no longer exist, simply because Beethoven's works no longer appear as questions in need of an answer – in other words, because how they are performed no longer seems to us a matter of much importance. When Wagner spoke of Beetho-ven, he became ecstatic – a fact received today with incredulity by those raised in the 'scientific' school of thought, who find that it tells them more about Wagner than about Beethoven. 'Ecstasy' is considered in any case an 'un-modern' way of responding to a work of art, appropriate rather to the Romantic nineteenth century that they have left behind.

One thing should be made clear at this point. The scientific and the artistic ways of looking at the world are fundamentally different, and can only exist side by side to a limited degree. At the same time neither can take precedence over the other and claim that it alone has the right to represent and govern the world. One would imagine that neither would advance such a claim. But this is not the case, for reasons which, when one looks into the matter, can be seen to lie in the nature of the two attitudes. The one seeks to live life, the other seeks to control it. The artist, who seeks life and nothing but life, gives himself over to his task in a totally different spirit from the scientist, who arranges and organizes, and assigns the artist his particular place. Sometimes it almost looks as though the artist is the quarry and the scientist the huntsman. Even this is a situation I am prepared to accept, for the artist has so perfect an opportunity to be himself, to revel in the joy of self-expression through his art, that others cannot but envy him. Yet if he is to leave any mark on the world, he is dependent on the response of that world. Which is where the scientist makes his appearance – intervening, however, in his own way, which is not the artist's. For do we not often get the impression today that the principles of how and what to compose, how and what to play, do not come from the artist himself at all? The man with the 'scientific' approach, the critic, the historian, may not be able to dictate to an audience but he has the general public under his thumb and is influential enough to lay down the law to the artist.

I mentioned above, à propos Beethoven, that attitudes towards the performance of music have changed. Our performances have lost a great deal of their freedom and spontaneity. They have become pondered and deliberate, down to the smallest detail, dominated by models and methodologies which often have not the remotest relevance to the works to which they are applied. The great works of the past depend to a large extent on intuition. But instead of being allowed to come to the fore in performance, this quality of intuition is played down, scorned. In fact, few people appear still to have any idea what the word means, and although the belief that everything can be learnt is now more widespread than ever, the real problems of performance, as they are and always have been, are often no longer recognized. Take, for instance, that of articulation, of phrasing, which can no more be prescribed in the notation than the inflexions of a great actor can be recorded in the printed text of a speech from Shakespeare. Liszt, in the Preface to his Symphonic Poems, was the first to give expression to this. 'Permit me to state,' he said,

> that I want to see an end to that dry, rigid, mechanical style of playing that is still commonly heard today. The only kind of performance I can accept is one based on natural phrasing, with proper attention given to the accents and to the delicate nuances of melody and rhythm.

Next to the problem of phrasing comes that of form, of structure, perhaps the most pressing question facing music today but one which we seem largely to have lost sight of. Besides this, the overly critical attitude encouraged by listening too often to radio and records, has led to soulless, mechanical, superficial performances, when what is needed is something quite different. To draw a parallel with art – it is like expecting to find the same close attention to fine detail that is part of the mastery of Dürer in pictures of a totally different style, such as those of Rembrandt or Titian. That there is an ideal of musical sound for every age, every composer, sometimes even every individual work, is a notion that has been lost sight of. On the contrary, such individualities are crushed under the weight of some rigid theory of literal, more 'stylish' performance, and the stupider and more primitive the theory, the more popular it becomes. Have we no idea how uncritical, how easily satisfied we have grown, and how boring our public musical life is becoming? If it is true, as I was recently told, that a young modern composer expressed the opinion, with a refreshing clarity, that the proper place for Mozart and Beethoven is a museum, and for Wagner, the rubbish dump, then it is a remark provoked by the present state of musical performance. Music has become divided into two types. On the one hand is the old music of the tonal era, the era which came to an end with Strauss, Ravel and the young Stravinsky and has been pronounced 'dead'; on the other hand is the New Music, which, as its supporters themselves admit, still lives more on its hopes than on its achievements.

Both on musical and historical grounds I know that this is not the way that natural developments come about. An art that was alive yesterday cannot be dead today, however many clever people tell us so. Likewise an art that was unable to displace an allegedly doomed art yesterday cannot do so today either, however desperately those same clever people wish it could. Since Nietzsche we have become accustomed to regarding our-selves – another aspect of the rise of science – as the measure of all things. But could not the reverse be equally true? Has Beethoven really failed us? Or have we perhaps failed Beethoven?

We are surrounded by examples of the disastrous effect of circumstances produced by intellectual argument, as opposed to experiential reality. In the past the press saw itself as forming a link between artist and public; the public's response was important to the critics, who used the work of art and its recep-tion to draw conclusions about the state of the arts in general. But in recent times these critics adopted a patronizing attitude and have taken to making up the public's minds for them. The view of the man in the street now counts for little – except as far as the impresario is concerned, who wants to ensure that the paying public turns up at the events he sponsors. Decisions on the quality of new compositions or on the skills of individual performers are taken without regard for the opinions of audi-ences.

This is strange, since an event like a concert or an opera is no less a shared, communal experience today than it always has been, and responsible critics have to report on it as such. Take those none-too-rare cases where an audience's reaction differs from those of the critics, with their fixed theories and principles. We are left with the impression that although there was an audience present – someone has to fill the hall – they have lost their right to an opinion. The immediate emotional impact of the music is being consistently played down, especially in Germany; indeed, it is often left out of account altogether, in response to new theories of composition. Musicians who follow this line totally reject 'emotional' music, like that of Wagner, for instance, and there are pianists – by no means the least capable – who refuse to play a note of Chopin for similar reasons.

What all such people fail to realize, and what the public at large seems unsure of, is that in a great work, as in a great performer, there can be no separation of mind and emotion. It is the performer's task both to turn the intellectual substance into an emotional experience and to convert the emotional content into an intellectual experience. There is no point in pursuing mind at the expense of emotion or *vice versa* – though we are surrounded by examples of precisely this. Wagner and Chopin would have been long since forgotten if they had done nothing else than offer us new forms of emotionality.

The most radical attempt at de-emotionalizing music is that made by composers using the so-called twelve-tone system. Here methodology – the backbone of science – has become all-important, while intuition and emotion – the hallmark of the artist – have all but vanished. That all we need today in order to create works of art is the proper methodology, is a notion which the much-maligned nineteenth century simply would not have understood. Examples like this go to show how profoundly our general attitudes have changed. Twelve-tone music is not only taken seriously by musicians and scholars but generally accepted without question. One side of the coin is to historicize, play down, devalue the music of the past; the other is to stake one's claims for a music of the future based on pre-stated theories and dogmas. The result is a totally different attitude to music, to art of all kinds. No longer is the artist a recipient of God's grace; no longer is his activity a source of awe and wonder. If he does not submit to the prevailing ideology, he is ignored, even attacked, regardless of who he is. I know a number of illustrious musicians who have no desire to return to their native Germany to find themselves branded as 'played-out Romantics'. Particularly tragic is the effect of this on the younger generation, who cannot find a position from which to start. Since critics and audiences proceed from such conflicting viewpoints, and therefore often come to such conflicting conclusions, young composers can make little headway.

The old twelfth-century argument between the nominalists and the realists, between the theorists whose desire is to define and control, and the artists, whose desire is to live, has been opened up again in the context of modern music. It is a struggle for supremacy in an age with a fanatical urge to theorize, an age in which science has become a religion. If we musicians do not wake up to the situation, music as an art, music as we know it, will quickly become a thing of the past. The struggle was spectacularly launched by Nietzsche in his pamphlet *The Case of Wagner*, since when it has grown in intensity from one decade to the next.

We dare not be under any illusion but that this is a matter of life and death for music, and that there is only one way to overcome the crisis. We cannot put the clock back. But nor can we content ourselves with vague hopes and demands. Our intelligentsia, which in the past has always pleaded the cause of what is vital and new, must become more intelligent, and instead of restricting itself to an aerial view of the state of music today, must descend to earth and see what is going on in the individual houses. By all means let our intellectuals use their historical perspective as a guide but not as a means of trying to control developments; they must learn to put the individual work of art, the phenomenon that is of direct concern to us, before matters of historical development. Above all, they must re-learn what it is to revere true greatness, to love it passionately, unreservedly, unconditionally. The situation is like that in Wagner's *Parsifal* – the only way to heal the wound is through the spear that caused it. The only way we can transcend the terrible effects of the warped thinking with which we are plagued is by recourse to a universal, all-embracing mode of thinking, thinking that moves on a higher plane. True art can flourish only in an atmosphere of naiveté, of spontaneity. Let us hope that all those in positions of responsibility will come to realize that this naiveté is the naiveté of wisdom, the recaptured naiveté that befits our mature civilization.

Notes

1 Concert Programmes

('Über Konzert-Programme', 1930)

1 Furtwängler uses the word *'Ereignis'* (the quotation marks are his), taken from the final chorus of Goethe's *Faust* and thereby calling on the philosophical associations both of that chorus and of the drama as a whole.

2 Principles of Interpretation

('Interpretation – eine musikalische Schicksalsfrage', 1934)

1 In the first scene of Wagner's *Siegfried*, Mime forges the sword Nothung, with which Siegfried slays the dragon Fafner, custodian of the Nibelung's ring.

3 The Tools of the Conductor's Trade

('Vom Handwerkszeug eines Dirigenten', 1937)

1 Arthur Nikisch (1855–1922) was the leading conductor of his day. He was appointed chief conductor of the Leipzig Gewandhaus Orchestra in 1895 and of the Berlin Philharmonic in 1897, both of which positions he held until his death. Reserved in his movements, seeming to hold his players in a spell by the force of his personality, he was the one conductor from whom Furtwängler was prepared to admit that he learned anything.
2 This is the theoretical background to Furtwängler's own inimitable technique, which to many outsiders seemed to produce a wavering and imprecise beat, especially at the opening of a piece. 'By beating out a figure, one destroys all feeling for the flow of the melody,'

169

he said. There is a story that, as he stood in front of the orchestra
with outstretched arms, holding everybody in suspense before the
first note of the piece, a voice shouted from the auditorium: '*Corag-
gio, Maestro!*'

4   Observations of a Composer

('*Bemerkungen eines Komponisten*', 1948)

Furtwängler wrote a considerable volume of music, very little of which
has been published. It stretches from his childhood years – piano
sonatas and chamber music – to a year or so before his death, when
he completed, but not fully revised, his Third Symphony. The bulk
of the surviving works belongs to a period down to about 1909; there
is then a gap until the 1930s, after which he concentrated on large-
scale forms, including a piano concerto and three symphonies (the
first of which he withdrew).

These observations were intended to accompany the first performance of his Second Symphony in E minor in 1948.

5   Bach
(1951)

1   The modern 'rediscovery' of Bach dates from Mendelssohn's
famous performance of the St Matthew Passion in Berlin in 1829.

6 Beethoven

a) Beethoven for Today

('*Anmerkungen zu Beethovens Musik*', 1918)

1   Goethe and Beethoven met in 1812. Beethoven, the younger by
twenty years, was the first great composer to be attracted to Goethe
– the Goethe, that is, of *Sturm und Drang*, author of *Götz von
Berlichingen* and *Werther*. His incidental music for the drama *Egmont*,
which Goethe completed in 1788, dates from 1809–10, and he also
set a number of his early lyrics. But by the time the two men met,
Goethe had left his *Sturm und Drang* world far behind and embraced
ideals of Classical poise and restraint which were the antithesis, as
he saw it, of all that Beethoven stood for. Hence his disapproving
reference to Beethoven's 'unruly nature' ('*ungebändigte Persönlich-*

keit'). In 1815 Beethoven composed a cantata on Goethe's 'Meeres-stille' and 'Glückliche Fahrt' of 1795, the two poems on which Mendelssohn – who was greatly admired by Goethe – based his concert overture of 1828. When the young Mendelssohn played Beethoven's Fifth Symphony to him in Weimar, Goethe described it as sounding 'as though the house was falling in'.

2 The inscription at the head of the third movement (in the Lydian mode) of Beethoven's String Quartet Opus 132.

3 *'Muss es sein? – Es muss sein!'* – the motto of the last movement of Beethoven's String Quartet Opus 135.

4 Wagner's most extensive piece of writing on Beethoven is his essay 'Beethoven' of 1870, from which Furtwängler's quotation comes. Throughout his life Wagner was at pains to emphasize the spiritual bond between himself and Beethoven.

5 From Goethe's conversations with Eckermann.

6 Beethoven's Opus 50 is the Romance in F for violin and orchestra, written in 1798.

b) The Universality of Beethoven

('Die Weltgültigkeit Beethovens', 1942)

1 From the choral finale of Beethoven's Ninth Symphony (*'Brüder – überm Sternenzelt/Muss ein lieber Vater wohnen'*).

c) Beethoven and Us. On the First Movement of Beethoven's Fifth Symphony

('Beethoven und wir. Bemerkungen über den ersten Satz der fünften Symphonie,' 1951)

1 The Austrian Felix Weingartner (1863–1942), who had studied with Liszt at Weimar, was a prolific composer of operas, symphonic and chamber music but is remembered chiefly as a conductor. He succeeded Mahler at the Vienna Court Opera in 1908. In addition to the book that Furtwängler mentions he wrote a practical hand-book on conducting (1895) and a study called *Die Symphonie nach Beethoven* (1906–18), from which Furtwängler quotes below.

2 The phrase occurs in Wagner's essay 'Beethoven' (1870).

3 The Hungarian folksongs which had such an influence on Bartók are themselves rich in irregular rhythms. In Stravinsky the *locus classicus* of irregular rhythms is *The Rite of Spring* (1913).

4 The Apollonian–Dionysian dichotomy in the culture of Classical Greece was posited by Nietzsche in his *Geburt der Tragödie* (1871).

5 From Goethe's poem 'Urworte. Orphisch'.
6 The influence of Goethe's concepts and thought-patterns can be felt throughout this essay. Words such as 'liberation' and 'purification' recall the principle of '*Stirb und werde*' – 'Die and be born again' – in the poem 'Selige Sehnsucht', the power of unceasing metamorphosis embedded in the processes of all organic life. The image of the organic evolution of man towards a state of harmony and perfection is also one to which Furtwängler has frequent recourse.
7 *Lamento e trionfo* is the sub-title of Liszt's symphonic poem *Tasso* (1849).
8 From Goethe's conversations with Eckermann. As often with Furtwängler, the form of his quotation strays some distance from the original.
9 From *Maximen und Reflexionen*.

7 Mendelssohn
(1947)

An address given in Leipzig to mark the centennial of Mendelssohn's death.

1 Uppermost in Furtwängler's mind in his appeal – one of many – for a return to traditional values is the break with those values embodied by twelve-tone music. In one of his diary jottings for 1945 he wrote: 'The step from Wagner to Schoenberg was a moment not of progress but of disaster. We are caught up in this disaster. The task before us is to return to the natural forces of growth and development'. In one of the last of these jottings occurs the sentence: 'Tonality is simply the structural organization of time'.
2 Mendelssohn was appointed conductor of the Leipzig Gewandhaus orchestra in 1835, at the age of twenty-six. As Royal Saxon Kapellmeister he was charged with the establishment of a music school, which opened its doors in April 1843. Among the first teachers engaged by Mendelssohn, the conservatoire's first director, was Schumann, who took classes in composition, score-reading and pianoforte.
3 Joseph Joachim, who became the greatest violinist of his age, was among the first students at the Leipzig conservatoire. As a fourteen-year-old boy he gave one of the earliest performances of the Mendelssohn concerto in 1845, and Brahms dedicated his concerto to him.
4 This famous performance took place in Zelter's *Singakademie* in Berlin on 11 March 1829. Mendelssohn was only twenty at the time. The famous actor Eduard Devrient, who helped Mendelssohn persuade Zelter to sanction the performance, recalled in his

memoirs that, as they came away from their successful mission, Mendelssohn cried out in delight: 'To think that it has been left to you, an actor, and me, a Jewish boy, to revive this greatest of all Christian music!'

5 Furtwängler's mode of thought stood in the tradition of German idealism, and he deliberately sets his 'category of naturalness' alongside the 'categories' of Kant.

6 For all his detestation of Nazism Furtwängler was a German through and through and could not but feel deeply humiliated by the defeat of 1945. He was always at pains to distinguish between the Germans and the Nazis, a distinction which at this moment (1947) many refused to draw. He never lost his sense of national pride. 'I am no politician,' he once said, 'but a representative of German music, which belongs to the whole of humanity.' In the immediate shadow of the holocaust the German-ness of the Jewish composers he mentions, alongside Mendelssohn, helps him to believe in the restoration of German honour.

8 Wagner

a) On the Music of Wagner's *Ring des Nibelungen*

('Anmerkungen zur Musik von Wagners Ring des Nibelungen', 1919)

These remarks were made on the occasion of a performance of Wagner's *Ring*, given in 1919 in Baden-Baden by the Mannheim opera, of which Furtwängler was then conductor. The post-war years saw a surge of anti-Wagner emotion, based not only on an aversion to the cult of megalomaniac Germanic values embedded in the subject matter but also on the extravagant Romanticism of Wagner's aesthetic means. Hence, on the one hand, Furtwängler's reference to the 'exaggerated Wagner-worship of an earlier age' but on the other, the need he feels to defend greatness against the fashionable scepticism represented by 'neo-Classicism' and related trends of the 1920s.

b) The Case of Wagner

('Der Fall Wagner, frei nach Nietzsche', 1941)

The title is an evocation of Friedrich Nietzsche's essay *Der Fall Wagner*, written in 1888, five years after Wagner's death.

1 *The Birth of Tragedy*, written in 1872, when Nietzsche was twenty-eight, casts Wagner as the Greek dramatist reborn, the genius

whose union of the arts under the supreme power of music proves
that the spirit of Greece still lives. This was the context in which
Wagner himself saw his historical role. But by 1876, the year of
the first Bayreuth Festival, Nietzsche had already begun to distrust
the values that Wagner stood for, and from having been his most
passionate admirer, he became his bitterest enemy, giving the most
violent expression to his hatred in *Der Fall Wagner*.

2   *Richard Wagner in Bayreuth* (1875–6) is Nietzsche's central work on
Wagner and shows him on the one hand still in the Master's grip
but on the other – when one reads between the lines – in a state
of confusion and unhappiness over the direction in which Wagner's
art was leading.

3   '*Götzendämmerung*' is Nietzsche's word.

4   A number of songs, choral and piano pieces by Nietzsche have
been published but a great deal of unpublished manuscript material
was destroyed in the Second World War.

5   cf. Furtwängler's remarks on *Carmen* in his essay on Bruckner (p.
110) and in *Form and Chaos* (p. 158).

6   The first line of a couplet used as a motto for the periodical *Kunst
und Altertum*, edited by Goethe and the painter Heinrich Meyer
('*Bilde, Künstler! Rede nicht! Nur ein Hauch sei dein Gedicht*').

7   The story of the love-sick hero of Goethe's epistolary novel *Die
Leiden des jungen Werthers* (1774) released a wave of sentimentality
throughout Europe the like of which had never been seen. Young
men unhappy in love affected the blue coat, yellow waistcoat and
top-boots that Werther wore and followed him in the suicide that
offered the only release from suffering.

8   This injunction reflected Goethe's alarm at the effects of his work
and his attempt to offset them, but it introduced a note of moral
didacticism alien to the spirit of the novel and the words were
never added to the text.

9   From the paralipomena to Schopenhauer's *Die Welt als Wille und
Vorstellung*.

9   Brahms

An address given before the German Brahms Society in May 1933 as
part of the centennial celebrations of Brahms' birth. Furtwängler was
the Society's Chairman.

1   The term *Neue Sachlichkeit* ('New Objectivity'), in use from the early
1920s onwards and originally applied to art and sculpture, came to
cover a variety of not always mutually compatible tendencies in
the art of the Weimar Republic. Underlying them, however, was a
common emphasis on the facts of life 'as it is' and a reaction in
the name of realism to the subjective bias of the Expressionists.

The *Gebrauchsmusik* associated with composers such as Hindemith, Hanns Eisler and Kurt Weill has its place in this context, as do current theories that art is for the people, not for a privileged élite, and that it is the duty of the artist to serve the needs of society at large. Furtwängler had little time for such campaigns. The artist's responsibility, he said, is to his art; by serving his art, he will automatically be serving society.

2 It was the critical remarks about Brahms made by Nietzsche and by Hugo Wolf that set the hostile tone of the relationship. Nietzsche characterized his music as expressive of 'the melancholy of impotence', while Hugo Wolf claimed that 'Brahms cannot rejoice.'

10 Bruckner
(1939)

1 Furtwängler's début as a conductor took place in Munich in 1906, when he conducted not only Bruckner's Ninth Symphony but also a composition of his own, an orchestral Adagio.

2 The history of the editions of Bruckner's symphonies is a complicated one. The earliest edition, instigated by Schalk and Löwe, to whom Furtwängler refers a few lines later, contains innumerable alterations to Bruckner's original text and is now hardly ever used. The International Bruckner Society charged Robert Haas with the task of removing the Schalk-Löwe accretions and restoring the symphonies to their original form; these were published between 1934 and 1944. Furtwängler seems to have been in two minds about the rival virtues of the two editions. In 1945 the International Bruckner Society commissioned Leopold Nowak to prepare yet another edition, in which the nine symphonies were published between 1951 and 1965.

3 August Halm was a composer and influential music educationalist whose theories stood in the shadow of Schopenhauer.

4 Hanslick frequently waxed scornful about Bruckner's music, his attitude, one suspects, being preconditioned by Bruckner's allegiance to Wagner.

5 Goethe is again in Furtwängler's mind: the 'grey area of theory' is that pointed to by Mephistopheles in his mocking scene with the Student in *Faust*:

> *Grau, teurer Freund, ist alle Theorie,*
> *Und grün des Lebens goldner Baum.*

> All theory, my friend, is grey,
> But green is the golden tree of life

11 Hindemith

('Der Fall Hindemith', 1934)

Published in the *Deutsche Allgemeine Zeitung* on November 25, 1934, this piece represents a public defence of Paul Hindemith against the preposterous racial attacks of the Nazis and their claims that he was a composer of 'degenerate' music. What angered Furtwängler was less the effect of these attacks on Hindemith himself than the arrogation to themselves by politicians of decisions that lay outside their competence and belonged in the sphere of artistic policy. Not surprisingly, after the publication of Furtwängler's letter Hitler banned the première of Hindemith's opera *Mathis der Maler*; Furtwängler and Hindemith had somehow combined to form an anti-Nazi symbol, recognized as such both by the public and by the Nazis. As a riposte to Hitler's action Furtwängler immediately resigned all his official posts.

1 The Amar Quartet, led by Licco Amar, was founded in 1921 and specialized in avant-garde music.
2 Szymon Goldberg was leader of the Berlin Philharmonic Orchestra from 1929 to 1934, when he emigrated to America.
3 Emanuel Feuermann taught at the Berlin Hochschule für Musik from 1929 to 1933; he went to the United States in 1938.
4 The short operas Furtwängler mentions belong to the years immediately following the First World War, and many found their part-expressionist, part-surrealist content tasteless and offensive. *Neues vom Tage* (1920) has a scene, which outraged Hitler, in which the heroine sings an aria while lying in the bathtub, where she is visited by the professional 'adulterer' hired to provide the 'evidence' necessary for her divorce. In the event he took his duties rather more seriously than his employers found appropriate.
    The *Badener Lehrstück*, so-called because it was written for the Baden-Baden Festival of 1929, has a didactic text by Brecht and includes, to the disgust of many, a scene in which two clowns saw off the limbs of a colleague one by one.
5 The opera *Mathis der Maler* was first performed in Zürich in 1938. The symphony of the same name, drawn from the music of the opera, was premièred under Furtwängler in March 1934, eight months before his public intervention on Hindemith's behalf.
6 The *Gebrauchsmusik* – 'music for use', 'practical music' – which Furtwängler mentions a few lines later is particularly associated with Hindemith and belongs in the general context of *Neue Sachlichkeit*, or 'Neo-Objectivity'. Hindemith's *Plöner Musiktag*, which Furtwängler mentions a few lines later, is a typical piece of *Gebrauchsmusik*. It seems strange that in his review of Hindemith's works Furtwängler makes no reference to his major achievement of the 1920s – the opera *Cardillac* (1926).

7 Apart from playing in chamber music ensembles, Hindemith was well-known in concerto work. He gave the first performance of Walton's Viola Concerto in 1929.
8 Hindemith's String Quartet No. 2 Opus 16 was written in 1921. It was specifically to play this work that the Amar Quartet was founded.
9 *Das Marienleben*, a cycle of songs to poems by Rainer Maria Rilke, composed in 1923.
10 Hindemith's comic opera *Neues vom Tage* parodies Wagner's *Tristan* in a scene (Act I, Scene 4) entitled 'Duet-Kitsch', which also mocks the 'grand opera' manner of Puccini. Furtwängler probably also had in mind the moment in Hindemith's one-acter *Nusch-Nuschi* when the hero is castrated to the accompaniment of the phrase to King Marke's anguished cry *'Dies, Tristan, mir?'* in *Tristan und Isolde*, when Marke discovers that he has been betrayed. (I am grateful to Geoffrey Skelton for helping me to track these references down).

12 Thoughts for All Seasons

('Zeitgemässe Betrachtungen eines Musikers', 1915)

1 The Czech composer Alois Hába (1898–1973) wrote pieces based on the division of the octave into quarter-tones and sixth-tones, and gave composition courses in these techniques at the Berlin Hochschule für Musik in the 1920s.
2 The tendency in Germany in the mid-nineteenth century was to confine the tempi and dynamics of a given piece to a comparatively narrow range, this being held to demonstrate its unity. Mendelssohn lent his authority to this practice. Wagner, by contrast, sought to uncover what he called the *melos*, the melodic essence, of every movement, every section, every phrase, which meant responding to the music more subtly, in greater detail, and consequently with a far greater variety of tempi, dynamics, timbres and so on. Apart from the intrinsic value of Furtwängler's observations, they have an interest as a comment on the practice of the time (1915) at which he was writing. He was in fact closer to the age of Wagner than we in 1990 are to him..

13 Open Letter to Dr Joseph Goebbels
(1933)

On 30 January 1933 Hitler was invited by President Hindenburg to become Chancellor of Germany. At that moment Furtwängler was on tour in Europe and England with the Berlin Philharmonic Orchestra.

Politics, he considered, should be left to politicians, and by the same token, music to musicians. He resented being told to get rid of the Jewish members of his orchestra just because they were Jewish: what mattered was their musicianship, not their religion. In March, the police in Leipzig locked the doors of the Gewandhaus to prevent Bruno Walter from conducting a concert that had been announced. On 12 April Furtwängler wrote his letter to Goebbels to protest against the anti-Semitic policies of the Nazis.

1   Bruno Walter and Otto Klemperer both left Germany in 1933 and spent the Second World War in the United States; Walter stayed there for the rest of his life (he died in 1962) but Klemperer returned to Europe in 1947 and died in Zürich in 1973. Max Reinhardt, who had had close links with America for many years, finally emigrated there from Austria in 1938 and died in New York in 1943.

14 Form and Chaos

('Chaos und Gestalt', 1954)

Furtwängler's remarks towards the end of the essay about the exercise of power in musical politics, and the one-sided results that it can produce, may bring a smile to the face of those who recall musical life in England in the 1960s and 1970s when William Glock was musical commissar of the BBC Third Programme.

1   Arthur Schnabel (1882–1951), Austrian by birth, taught in Berlin until 1933, when, as a Jew, he was forced into exile. He settled in America in 1939 but returned to Europe after the Second World War. As a pianist, he was especially known for his performances of Beethoven, Schubert and Brahms. His compositions, among them a symphony, a piano concerto, chamber and instrumental pieces, are atonal in character.
2   The 'I–Thou' terminology stems from the Jewish philosopher Martin Buber. God is the great 'Thou', and it is the individual's relationship to this great 'Thou' that makes possible the 'I–Thou' relationships between man and man, which in their turn presuppose an encounter with the fullness of being on both sides – an encounter between two sovereign subjective entities. In the aesthetic context in which Furtwängler uses the terminology, 'I–Thou' stands for the creative relationship between artist and public.
3   It is customary to describe as 'atonal' Schoenberg's revolutionary Three Piano Pieces Opus 11 (1908) and Six Small Piano Pieces Opus 19 (1911); his twelve-tone compositions came in the 1920s, starting with the Piano Suite Opus 25 (1924).
4   Furtwängler will have had in mind works like Hindemith's surreal-

ist one-act operas *Mörder, Hoffnung der Frauen* (libretto by Kokosch-ka) and *Das Nusch-Nuschi*, the *Kammermusik* No. 1 and the song-cycle *Das Marienleben*, and Ernst Křenek's first three string quartets.

5   The most important works by Bartók in the early post-First World War years are the two violin sonatas, the *Dance Suite* and *The Miraculous Mandarin*. Stravinsky's *L'histoire du soldat* was written in 1918, and was followed by the *Symphonies of Wind Instruments, Pulcinella* and *Mavra*.

15 'Greatness is Simplicity'

('Alles Grosse ist einfach', 1954)

1   The Demonic (*das Dämonische*) in Goethe connotes the unique and ultimately irresistible force in each individual that drives him towards his preordained destiny, however much, recognizing its potentially destructive power, he may struggle against it. Charac-ters such as Faust and Egmont in Goethe's plays show the principle being lived out in practice, as does Werther in his novel *Die Leiden des jungen Werthers*, whom Furtwängler draws into his discussion of Wagner and Nietzsche in his essay 'The Case of Wagner' (p. 66ff above).

Index